ONE MAN'S JOURNEY

WITH A SILENT PARTNER

ONE MAN'S JOURNEY

WITH A SILENT PARTNER

Charles F. Remaley Jr.

MOUNTAIN ARBOR
PRESS

Mountain Arbor
Press
Alpharetta, GA

The author has tried to recreate events, locations, and conversations from his memories of them. In some instances, in order to maintain their anonymity, the author has changed the names of individuals and places. He may also have changed some identifying characteristics and details such as physical attributes, occupations, and places of residence.

ISBN: 978-1-63183-129-4

Library of Congress Control Number: 2017911864

10 9 8 7 6 5 4 3 2   0 8 0 7 1 7

Printed in the United States of America

♾This paper meets the requirements of ANSI/NISO Z39.48-1992 (Permanence of Paper)

Photographs are from Charles F. Remaley Jr. and Carol Remaley Johnson's family collections.

Permission for image of Navy Log granted by the Director of the Navy Log, United States Navy Memorial, Washington, DC.

For PFC Norman Arthur Uhleman (1924–1944)
In memory of the soldier whose life was lost in the invasion of Leyte,
Philippines, during World War II.

Acknowledgments

It is with gratitude that I thank the following for their support and encouragement:

To my friends at the Rosedale United Methodist Church, the Presbyterian Senior Care "the Willows" division, the Oakhurst Tea Room, the Country Kitchen, the La Café, the men of Arby's, my neighbors, my medical community supporters, my nieces and nephews, and my sister, Audrey, who passed away in February 2017.

To my son, Bob, who has always shown a great interest in my Navy days, generously shared his historical WWII knowledge with me, and attended many *LST-1024* reunions with Jean and me over the years. And a special thank-you to my daughter, Carol Johnson, who reinitiated my efforts to complete this book through her 2014 Father's Day gift—the typed partial manuscript of my early efforts, complete with photos. From seven hundred miles away, she has continued to type my ongoing handwritten manuscript for many months as I resumed writing my story and has coordinated with others to bring this book to print.

To the publishing team at Mountain Arbor Press for their personal and professional support.

CHARLES F. "RED" REMALEY JR.

BOSTON, MA 1944

RATE/RANK

MOMM2

SERVICE BRANCH

USN 9/1943 - 5/1946

BORN

10/19/1925
VERONA, PA

NAVY LOG

SIGNIFICANT DUTY STATIONS

NAVAL TRAINING CENTER, GREAT LAKES, IL
DIESEL SCHOOL, NAVY PIER, CHICAGO, IL
USS LST-1024
LEYTE, LINGAYEN GULF, OKINAWA

SIGNIFICANT AWARDS

AMERICAN CAMPAIGN MEDAL
ASIATIC PACIFIC CAMPAIGN MEDAL W/3 STARS
WORLD WAR II VICTORY MEDAL
NAVY OCCUPATION SERVICE MEDAL (ASIA)
PHILIPPINE LIBERATION MEDAL W/2 STARS

Introduction

As the years pass, I reflect more and more about the things that have happened in my life. Many of my reflections are on the time spent in the Navy during World War II, but that was not my whole life. I had a childhood and a wonderful life following the time I spent serving my country. Life is so full of wonderful things, as well as some disappointments, but overall, life is what you make of it.

"You should write a book," I heard so many times throughout my life, after relating some of the instances during those days in the Navy. When I was a child, I had no "big dreams" about the future, especially after December 7, 1941, when the Japanese attacked Pearl Harbor. I was sixteen years of age when that happened, and I enlisted in the Navy before my eighteenth birthday. When I left high school I stated I would never open another book, let alone write one. If I should finish writing this book, you will discover that this statement did not hold much water.

If my writings turn into a book, you will read only truths, no exaggerations or defamations. There will be humor, romance, and serious reflections upon many happenings in my life. This will be a story about one man's journey with a "Silent Partner." There have been times when I walked with God and times when I did not, but through it all He never deserted me.

I take pen in hand at the urgings of many, but especially those of my family. This work would not have reached completion without the aid of my daughter, Carol Johnson, who has already done a masterful job of setting me on course to be a reluctant author.

Charles "Red" F. Remaley Jr.
June 2016

The Beginning

It was early morning on July 5, 1944. There was a slight mist upon the waters of New York Harbor, the sun was just rising above the eastern horizon, and the city skyline was beginning to glow as the sun's rays played upon the towering buildings off the port bow of our ship, the USS *LST-1024*. Ours was one of many ships at anchor in New York Harbor, and all due preparation was being made for us to join a convoy to an unknown destination, at least unknown to those of us among the noncommissioned personnel. We had returned to this port the day before, Independence Day — a day when it was traditional to set off fireworks—but such a tradition was the farthest thing from our minds. We had just come in from the "ammunition dump" in Leonardo, New Jersey, and our cargo was 100 percent ammunition.

On this getaway day, many thoughts of past and future experiences dominated my mind as the main engines revved up deep within the ship's bowels. As an eighteen-year-old, I was at the divide between boyhood and manhood, and regardless of my feelings, I was not in control of my destiny. Separation from family was a very real experience, but I was fortunate to have had a day of liberty in late June, on which I joined my mother and sister for a day on the town, which had included a trip to the top of the Empire State Building.

I am from Verona, a small town in western Pennsylvania, a suburb of Pittsburgh. As in most small towns, not too much exciting ever happens, but we are a close community with an emphasis on sports in season. I suppose the most memorable thing to happen in our town was the tragic 1936 flood, which brought the waters of the Allegheny

River onto Main Street. The water was so deep that traffic consisted solely of power boats, and many homes were covered completely.

How prepared is anyone about to travel that first mile toward a war that was already several years old? With a "prepare for war" mentality, many of us in high school were sent off to trade school to learn a trade that would be helpful in the war effort. I studied auto mechanics, which opened the way for diesel school at Navy Pier in Chicago following boot camp at Great Lakes Naval Training Base in Illinois. Along with my schooling at Navy Pier, I gained an insight to the marvelous care and concern the people of Chicago had for those in the military. They could not do enough to please you. One incident that warms my heart occurred as I walked up to an intersection in the heart of town where an officer was directing traffic.

I was about to step off the curb when the officer shouted, "Hold it right there!"

As he walked toward me I wondered what I had done to gain his attention, when he spoke again: "I wonder if you would do me a favor?"

This only added to the mystery. He proceeded to tell me that in the middle of the next block, in the direction I was traveling, there was an organization of women who had gone to great lengths to make things for people in the military, and he wanted me to pay them a visit. I assured him I would do him that "favor." I came out of that welcome house with a full stomach, a hand-knitted scarf, and a tossle hat. Such love and helpfulness abounded everywhere I went in that great city.

In addition to our schooling at the pier, we spent time each day doing physical training in the gymnasium. One of the drills was to carry another person on your back—it did not matter if he was twice your size. In the course of that drill, I severely injured my back, but received only five heat treatments during off hours. This was an injury that would plague me the rest of my life.

Diesel school went well and I developed some friendships with the other students. One of these friends was Bob Renner, the son of a coal baron from southern Illinois. He was a fine young man, and we went on liberty on several occasions. Prior to one of these outings, he asked if I had ever played table tennis. I quickly answered that I was a high school champ, which was a total fabrication that I intended to own up to—except it slipped my mind. Well, on liberty we went to the USO, for they always had so much to do. Before I knew it, we each had a paddle in our hand and Bob was ready to serve. *Wham!* The ball sailed past my head so fast that I thought it would take my ear off.

"You lying SOB!" Bob shouted. He figuratively undressed me.

I learned a lesson that day. Bob never ceased to tease me about my game. One day his mother came to one of Chicago's finer hotels and invited Bob and me to dine with her in her room. If ever a small-town boy felt out of his element, it was I. It was like a scene out of a movie as the waiter rolled that huge cart into her room and began to set up the dinner. I had never seen so much fancy tableware. I didn't know which utensil to use, but I did make it through the meal. For just a moment, I was a millionaire.

Our days at diesel school came to a close after three months, ending on the last of February 1944. We had our sad farewells and went our separate ways. One friend Paul Retherford, like me, was assigned to amphibious training at Camp Bradford, Virginia. During that training, we were formed into crews to serve aboard LSTs. Paul went to a different crew and I lost track of him. Gradually, new friendships developed in this new assignment, and day by day we became more than friends. We became shipmates, but shipmates without a ship.

The need for a ship was soon to be supplied. We were loaded onto a train, which from the outside looked like old boxcars. Inside, we were exposed to the dingiest accommodations on wheels I had ever seen. There were bunks four high running from side to side as opposed to being parallel to the tracks. It was a night train to Boston, a ride I will never forget. However, after the war I saw many pictures of those trains that Hitler loaded with Jews on their way to prison camps and gas chambers, people not lying down, but standing so tightly together that they could not even fall. So what do I have to complain about?

Upon our arrival in Boston, we were quartered in the Fargo Building, which to us was like a hotel after those drafty tents in Virginia. We went to the shipyard daily to be familiarized with the *LST-1024*, which was nearing completion and would be our home until the end of the war and beyond.

Boston, like Chicago, had a warm heart for our nation's servicemen and women. While at the Fargo Building I bumped into Al Honsperger, a man I had known back home since the age of three. He too was waiting for his ship to be completed. I saw him almost every day, and we took some liberty together in town. One Sunday morning, we waited at the trolley stop so we could attend church. Before a trolley came along, a car came to a halt right in front of us. The window rolled down and a man asked if we needed a ride into town. Of course we did. We hopped in and headed toward our destination. The man asked where we were going so early in the morning. When we told him, he said it was too early for church, and since we were strangers in town, he would be happy to give us a tour of his city and then drop us off at a church when it was the proper time. He delighted us with tours of college campuses, Old North Church, and Boston Commons. What fond memories I have of that man's kindness, and that of others in the city of Boston. Shortly after that Sunday together, Al and I went to sea on our respective ships. We went to Chesapeake Bay for our shakedown cruise and then to New York Harbor.

Word was now being passed that we were about to get underway. As the anchor detail was getting set to weigh anchor, I looked out across the bow and saw the most awesome ship I had ever seen. It was enormous and flat gray in color, and it moved slowly as harbor tugboats took their places alongside to guide that enormous hulk into a berth along one of those piers that juts out into the harbor. The ship was soon identified as the *Queen Elizabeth*, a peacetime luxury liner turned troop ship, which explained its dull gray color. We assumed it was just returning after taking troops to Europe where just a month ago the Allies had made a major invasion at Normandy with great loss of life and heavy casualties. They called it "D Day."

On Our Way:
Cuba, Panama, San Diego

Anchors aweigh! We were slowly moving to take up our assigned position in a convoy of ships moving out to sea. Once underway we were informed that our first port of call would be Guantanamo Bay, Cuba. As we moved outward from the harbor I looked back at a lady with her right arm raised high in the sky. That "lady" was the Statue of Liberty, and I shall never forget the sight of her fading away as we moved out toward the Atlantic Ocean.

Prior to taking on our cargo, we had several days of liberty in New York City and were required to be back on board each night. Everyone obeyed that order until one night, Nick—I will not identify him further—did not return. The captain was furious, since it was too late to replace those who deserted the ship. The following day, Nick showed up and was quickly hauled before the captain. Of course, the captain wanted an explanation, so Nick, whose home was in nearby Brooklyn, told him he had spent the time with his wife trying to make a baby.

"Dismissed," the captain said.

Nine months later, Nick announced a new arrival.

Any group of people is made up of some who stand out for one reason or another. Everett Chase was one of those. His forte was to drive people crazy with his make-believe dog, Freddie. Chase would walk into a bar while calling and scolding Freddie for not following close to his heels. Other patrons would turn and look everywhere for that dog, which was not permitted on the premises. They looked in vain as Chase took his place on a bar stool and then called for Freddie to join him on an adjacent stool. He would always get a frown from the bartender, but Chase would ignore him while asking the dog what he wanted to drink. Then he would look at the bartender and order two identical drinks, telling him one was for Freddie. All the while he carried on a conversation with the dog, closing it out with, "Freddie, if you are not going to drink that I will drink it for you." He would down the second drink, turn, and walk toward the door, then say, "Come on, Freddie, let's get out of here," to the laughter of those around him. I tell this story because our ship's mascot was named Freddie as a tribute to Everett Chase, one of our ship's cooks.

As we headed southward along the coast, the waters began to get a little rough, and I thought about a practice shakedown cruise we had taken on another LST several weeks ago. Before leaving port on that cruise, Max Bridges had awed us with stories that made him out to be quite a seagoing salt. Well, about halfway between Boston and Norfolk, Virginia, I saw him in the crew's head sitting on one commode and throwing up in another. He was so seasick he could not move, and by the time we got to Norfolk, it was decided that this "old salt" was not cut out for sea duty. He was promptly separated from our crew.

A couple of days at sea brought our crew closer to the routine and discipline that would be our fare throughout the remainder of the war. None of us was an expert at anything, and few of us had any real experience at our jobs. It took a while for the cooks and bakers to get used to preparing meals for over 125 men. Remember, these men were not cooks or bakers in civilian life. I, along with many others, was not too happy with those first few meals, but I was unable to do aboard ship what I had done at Camp Shelton in Virginia, when I would get so disgusted with the poor meals that I would climb a fence separating Camp Shelton from Camp Bradford and join their chow line for a good meal. It was the only time I was ever AWOL.

As a member of the "Black Gang," a designation assigned to those of us who worked below deck, four hours duty and eight hours off became routine while at sea. The eight hours off were not meant for leisure, as we had other diverse maintenance duties outside of our two engine rooms. Knowing my shipboard assignments would always be below deck bothered me at first, but it became something I got used to as time passed. Of course, during general quarters I was part of a four-man crew on a forty-millimeter antiaircraft gun, so I knew I would be topside during battle conditions. In addition to my schooling as a diesel mechanic, I had also spent some time at gunnery school, which proved to be among my most embarrassing moments. We had been learning how to shoot at a sleeve towed by an aircraft at an appropriate height. One day as I was being instructed on how to use a twenty-millimeter antiaircraft gun, the plane came in overhead. I was awaiting the command to fire, when the instructor asked me what I had in my gun sight. *Gulp*—it was the plane!

Just when we were getting used to our routine at sea, we arrived in Guantanamo Bay. We all began to feel like old salts because we could brag about having been to a foreign port. Little did we realize how many other foreign ports lay ahead of us. I was immediately intrigued by the pelicans hovering in the air all around us. They chose a target in the water, dropped like a bomb upon an unsuspecting fish, then flew away to consume their meal.

Our stay in Cuba was brief, but not without drama. All was peace and quiet, and those not on watch were fast asleep when the alarm for general quarters sounded at about 0200 hours. At first blink, we wondered if we were under attack, but with little time to get dressed and off to our battle stations, we stumbled in the darkness to our assigned positions. The main engines started up and the anchor detail was activated. Then we were informed that our ship's anchor was not holding against the changing tide and we were drifting rapidly toward another ship. With our cargo of ammunition, we did not need a scientist to explain the imminent danger. It took only a few minutes to haul up the anchor and get those twin screws spinning to get us out of danger. We moved to a new anchorage, but maintained a special watch for the rest of the night.

Upon leaving Cuba, we were informed that our next port would be Colon, Panama. We immediately encountered rough seas, so rough that our flat bottom LST was tossed like a cork on the water. The ship rolled from side to side, waves pouring onto the deck with each roll. I managed to keep my food down for most of the first day, and then I went into my impersonation of the "old salt," Max Bridges, who probably was somewhere laughing at the world. The ship's railing was becoming my favorite place to be, so long as I chose a location where the wind was not blowing toward me. Of course, there were still all those watches to stand in the engine room along with other chores to be done. Oh, how I wished I were somewhere else. Being sick was bad enough, but my engineering officer, Mr. Nichols, was constantly on my back for being such a weakling in the face of rough weather. Just after my last episode at the rail, I pulled back quickly and caught my dog-tag chain on the post and watched helplessly as those tags flew off into the sea. Amid my exasperation over losing my dog tags, I looked into the face of my other tormenter, Mr. Nichols, who still could not understand my problem.

Other than car sickness, I had had only one occasion when such sickness had come upon me. It happened on a weekend pass while in diesel school when I flew from Chicago to Pittsburgh via Dayton and Columbus, Ohio. We were not aloft long when I explained to the stewardess that I was in trouble. She gave me a container to help my cause. By the time we got to Columbus I needed to freshen up, and the stewardess said I could hurry into a restroom during the brief layover. While hurrying through my cleanup, I mentioned to a gentleman that I was hurrying so the plane would not take off without me. He said, "Don't worry about it, I am the pilot."

About three days into our voyage to Panama, I had an urgent need to speak with Mr. Nichols. I could not find him. I asked the others in our division where he was and got the same answer from each that they had not seen him. We were not supposed to go into officer's country on board the ship, but I felt my business was urgent, so I knocked on Mr. Nichols's stateroom door and heard a weak response to come in. There was my tormenter slouched in his bed, too seasick to even answer the knock upon his door. I did not have to wonder why he left me alone during the remainder of that five-day trip.

With five days of rough seas behind us, we made port in Panama, to the relief of many weary men. It was so calm and peaceful under a blazing sun and waving palm trees. It was such a relief to set foot on solid ground. We were permitted generous liberty while awaiting our turn to go through the canal. On one of those liberties, I happened to be in the major PX in Colon when a big tropical storm suddenly came up. This was my first experience with such weather. I was so glad I was indoors, but I still feared the building would collapse. There was an eerie calm within that building, when there came this thunderous noise from the main entrance, which sounded like a runaway jeep coming through the doors. Incredibly, all that noise had been made by one man, who must have been running full speed when he hit those doors. This man looked like someone who had been out fishing in a storm, for he was dressed in a long, black, rubber raincoat with a matching hat. He got our attention as he took off that fisherman's hat and slammed it against his side to expel the water. What a shock I got when I recognized him as my former classmate at Navy Pier, Paul Retherford. It was not only a surprise, but a great reunion.

During our short stay in Panama, we got the tragic news that an ammunition ship had exploded in Pittsburg, California, with great loss of life. Being on an ammunition ship ourselves this kind of news did little for our morale, and we looked forward to the day when our cargo would be discharged.

We sure got a look at the seamy side of life as we walked the streets of Colon, Panama. I had never been exposed to such loose living and vulgarity as I witnessed in that town. In the months ahead, I was to learn how commonplace these observations would be. Perhaps this had always been a way of life along the sea. The quiet decency of the small town of my boyhood was pleasant and comforting to remember.

In the evening of our third day in Panama, we received orders to proceed toward the canal and the first set of locks. It was an exciting time for us all, as a trip through the canal had been but a dream when studying geography in grade school. It was now coming to pass; it would no longer be a dream but a reality to be set in our memory banks forever. Shortly after passing through the first set of locks, darkness began to fall, so we were denied the marvel of the Panama Canal. Thus, our passage was accomplished in darkness, but we would have missed some of the sights anyway from standing watch in the engine rooms.

As dawn was breaking, we entered the Pacific Ocean. It was never a mystery as to which ocean would be our theater of operation because our ship, from the beginning, was painted in camouflage — colors that would blend with the coloring found in the islands of the Pacific. It was ugly, but it made sense. We were at battle stations that morning, which became our routine every dawn and dusk throughout the war. These were the best times for enemy planes to attack, with the rising or setting sun at their backs.

As we looked into the western sky, the rising sun was at our back and reflecting in all its glory against a cloud formation that resembled a port city, with piers jutting into the harbor and ships coming and going. Without the sun, I doubt these clouds would have gotten our attention, but with it we observed a golden city in the heavens the likes of which I had never seen before or since. Only God could paint a picture like that.

Moving out of the canal area and into the open sea, we turned northwest, which took us along the western coast of Mexico. Our port of call would be San Diego, California. This was a beautiful trip in calm waters and good weather, and the highlight of the trip was watching a school of dolphins off the starboard bow, heading north like we were. It proved to be the only sighting of these beautiful creatures that I would ever see.

San Diego was to be a one-day affair, giving us only enough time to take on a load of troops. Some crewmen got a brief liberty, but most of us remained on board. I had always wanted to go to California, but when I got there I could not even set foot on its soil.

First Stop, Pearl Harbor

With San Diego several days behind us, we were still in convoy heading for Hawaii. Along the way, we had opportunity to practice our gunnery skills by shooting at large balloons released into the air. Our gun crew got credit for shooting down one balloon. As a crew, we worked well together, and I was confident we could meet the challenge when real battle conditions came our way.

One night, about a week out from San Diego, there was a Japanese submarine alert and we got orders to scatter. After several hours, the all clear was sounded and we had to reform our convoy. Getting all those ships back together in the dark took some doing, but in time it was accomplished. For those responsible for navigating port to port, my hat was off. I could not get over how well they did their job. So many places across the broad Pacific were but the tiniest of specks on a map but we always made it to our assigned destination.

On our twelfth day out of San Diego, the island of Oahu came into view. Our ship was so slow that it seemed we never had to slow down, since our top speed was only twelve knots. We did, however, move slowly into Pearl Harbor because it was such a busy place. We were directed to an anchorage where the closest thing to us was the sunken, rusting hulk of the USS *Arizona*, which was sunk in the Japanese sneak attack on the US Pacific Fleet on Sunday, December 7, 1941. To look out upon this once-proud battleship so totally destroyed and entombing more than a thousand men of the US Navy was a sad sight to behold. It was only fitting that in later years it would become one of our nation's most recognized and revered memorials.

suffer one way or another. Well, one day while he was returning from another two-beer liberty in Honolulu, he was in such a stupor that he tumbled backward from the liberty boat's aft deck and into the water. As he sank beneath the surface our gunnery officer, who was officer of the deck that day, dove over the rail from the main deck into the murky water and brought him to the surface, where he was aided in getting him shipboard. He was a survivor and never changed his habit of drinking. As a result, we nicknamed him "Two-Beer Tracey." He survived the war.

We received orders to leave Pearl Harbor and proceed to the island of Maui. We arrived on September 1, 1944, and soon learned we would be loading up with combat troops along with all their gear and mechanized equipment, which consisted of amphibious troop carriers and amphibious tanks. All these huge vehicles were backed aboard so that they could be discharged easily once we neared the beach. However, before that heavy equipment came into our tank deck, they brought enough seventy-five-millimeter shells, packed three to a crate, that they made a three-foot layer of ammunition underneath all those vehicles. It surely brought back memories of the load we brought from New Jersey.

It took nearly a week to get everything loaded and stowed in the most efficient manner, along with billeting the troops in living compartments below deck. For the size, an LST was a super ship in the sense that it could carry such a large cargo as well as large numbers of troops, and unload with exceptional speed.

While at Maui, we got in a lot of swimming off the bow ramp and off the port side near the quarter deck, where swimming was somewhat hazardous to your health if you were too close to the ship when someone flushed a toilet. We had to make like a submarine—you know, "Dive! Dive!" Speaking of diving, it was not my strong suit, but there was our deck officer diving off the overhead above the quarter deck, perhaps a drop of twenty feet. I could not stand seeing him do that without challenging him. The moment I was airborne, I felt I had made a mistake. The moment I hit the water, I was sure of it. What a headache! It felt like someone had replaced the water with solid ground. I did not make a second dive.

While swimming alongside the ship, the current seemed to shift rapidly, and one man began moving away from the ship, slowly at first, then he was so far out that he could not get back to safety and was fast losing strength. A nearby shipmate dove into the water when the rescue line fell short, and he swam to the rescue, holding the man's head above the water. By this time, both men had been pulled a great distance from the ship. Fortunately, one of our small boats was made ready in time to save both men. The next day, the shipmate who had gone to the rescue was hospitalized with acute appendicitis and was lost to our crew.

Heading to the
South Pacific: Eniwetok, Manus

Fully loaded, we returned to Pearl Harbor with our battle-ready cargo of men and equipment. Within two days, we were joined with other ships, similarly loaded and forming a convoy for the next invasion on the island-hopping course that would eventually lead to Japan. On September 11, 1944, we moved out to sea and toward our destination, the invasion of the island of Yap, which is southwest of Guam and east of the Philippines. While traveling toward our target, the joint chiefs of staff huddled together with the news that late information on strengths and weaknesses in the Japanese forces in the Philippines could dictate a major change in strategy. Shortly thereafter, we got word that the Yap invasion was cancelled and that we would put in at Eniwetok, an island west of the Marshall Islands that had been won over in February 1944.

On course toward Eniwetok, we crossed the International Date Line, which puts you into tomorrow if you are traveling west, and yesterday if you are going east. This crossing took place on September 18, 1944, and made all hands members of the Imperial Domain of the Golden Dragon. We were each presented with a membership card signed by the captain. We arrived without incident in Eniwetok on September 25 for only an overnight stay, but it was long enough to have a mail delivery, which was always a highlight. Two weeks of mail had accumulated, and I got lots of letters. I can't remember hitting any port where mail was not there waiting for us, a remarkable achievement. Reading through my mail, a letter from my mother informed me of her father's death — this was the grandfather mentioned earlier, and the one my friend Jack had visited in Ohio.

By this time, the troops on board had been with us three weeks, and with the canceling of the Yap invasion, it was obvious they would be on board for some time to come. We developed a strong fellowship through the weeks, as we all shared the same facilities for showers, shaving, and creature comforts. Over time I became better acquainted with a soldier named Art. When I look back on short-lived friendships, I think about how little we ever divulged about our personal lives. Our conversations were mostly about today and the encounter that lay ahead. Art was billeted in the compartment next to mine, so we exchanged pleasantries as well as barbs many times over the weeks.

On September 26, we left Eniwetok for Manus, which is in the Admiralty Islands just south of the equator, a place won over from the Japanese in March 1944. On our way south we, of course, crossed that great divide called the equator, and traditionally the "shellbacks," those who have already crossed the line, administer some form of initiation. Fortunately, there were not many shellbacks on board, so we escaped with some mild paddling, but we got our shellback membership cards on October 4 just before reaching Manus.

Arriving in Manus was shocking to us. As we maneuvered into this vast anchorage, there was before us an armada of ships of all sizes and classes in numbers beyond our imagination. There were capital ships, supply ships, and amphibious ships of all sorts. That anchorage was well protected by the reefs that surrounded it. However, if there were enough Japanese aircraft within striking distance, this could have been a disaster worse than Pearl Harbor, like shooting fish in a barrel. Fortunately, no air attacks were forthcoming, so we concentrated on reading our mail and keeping up with preparations for the invasion, which we were primed for and knew was close at hand. I had reason to believe that a cousin of mine was stationed in Manus, but I was not able to locate him.

The longer we were at sea, the more bugs we got in our bread. Even sifting the flour did not help the situation. It was standard procedure for us when we entered the mess hall to hold each slice of bread up to the light, and if there were not too many bugs, we ate it. On a bad day, the GI can by the scullery where we emptied our trays would be full of discarded bread. When the bakers began baking raisin bread, we were deeply suspicious. Following the war, I had occasion to ride some distance on a train with a former soldier who had been held in a Japanese prison camp after his capture. One thing I will always remember is what he told me about bugs in his prison cell—he caught and ate them to supplement his meager rations. What is so bad about a few well-cooked bugs in a full slice of bread?

A week passed quickly at Manus as we made our final preparations for battle, which we now knew would be an invasion of the Philippines. The target would be the island of Leyte, which was in an east-central part of the island group. Not knowing when or where we would have access to a supply depot, we loaded maximum food for crew and troops. In addition to our own fuel supply, we were required to fill other storage tanks for refueling small escort vessels at sea such as destroyer escorts and sub chasers.

Refueling began with our deck crew tossing a line to the ship needing fuel, then pulling it back after it was attached to their refueling hose. This operation always went well, but on one occasion the sea had swells so large that the ship alongside us would almost disappear when a swell rose between us. Refueling was serious business and dangerous because of the possibility of collision. However, at one refueling, I stood and watched in amusement as our "experienced" deck hands could not get a line to the other ship. Several men had tried unsuccessfully at tossing that monkey ball to the other ship, so amid their frustration I asked if I could try it. With doubtful stares, they handed me the line, and after coiling it I twirled the monkey ball and let it fly. It reached the target. Mission accomplished! Some people are just lucky.

Invasion of the Philippines: Leyte Gulf

By October 13, we were some distance north of New Guinea, having left Manus in a monstrous convoy on October 11, 1944, heading for Leyte. It would not surprise me if someone said there were five hundred ships in the convoy. Everything went well considering how crowded the ship had been with troops, crew, and cargo since the first week in September. There was a lot of good-natured banter between the Army and Navy, and we got better acquainted with those quartered nearby, including my friend Art, who was an infantry scout, a hazardous position.

The date for the invasion of Leyte was set for October 20, and it was fast approaching. From the seventeenth of October, the Japanese seemed quite sure that Leyte would be targeted, because they had become aware of US Navy minesweepers along our intended route in the Leyte Gulf clearing a path for the giant convoy that had gained in size since MacArthur's forces had joined us on the move northward. Ahead of our arrival at Leyte were ranger units working the shorelines of those islands facing our advancing convoy and a special collection of six old battleships pounding the shores closer in. This group was under the command of Admiral Oldendorf. General MacArthur's command ship was the USS *Nashville*, which was still some forty-eight hours from the targeted area, and the overall protection of this vast undertaking was the responsibility of the Third and Seventh Fleets of the US Navy.

On October 19, under the cover of darkness, we moved cautiously through the straits leading into Leyte Gulf. This was my nineteenth birthday and had to be the most awesome one in my life. As we wended our way through those outer islands, we could see small, red guiding lights along the shore, which were placed and maintained by the rangers. These lights enhanced our confidence for the battle ahead, though our anxiety was running high. Before the light of dawn, we could hear the battleships and other supporting ships pounding the shoreline where we were to make our landing. As dawn broke, the sky was filled with a layer of smoke from the ships' guns and exploding shells on the beach. Higher up, there were puffs of smoke from exploding shells being fired at the few marauding Japanese planes that had ventured in over the invading forces. We had been at battle stations from the wee hours of the morning, ready for whatever came our way. Nobody could have slept that night anyway.

As the shelling increased, our chief cook took off for sanctuary below deck. In fact, he shut himself in the walk-in food cooler. We did not know why he responded in that way until later in the day when we learned he had been a victim of Pearl Harbor, not physically wounded, but emotionally. This became his routine at the height of battle, and he had our deepest sympathies. He was a good shipmate and had no qualms about staying aboard.

As we closed toward the beach area where the landing was to be made, we came to a stop, as did the other LSTs in our group. As I stated earlier, the heavy equipment we had on board, the troop carriers and tanks, were amphibious and could reach the beach from several hundred yards out in reasonably calm waters. Only when we came to a stop did we learn that we would discharge these vehicles off the bow ramp some distance from shore.

From early September until this day of the invasion, we had not seen our Army guests in their battle gear, but now reality was setting in for them and for us, as they had battle helmets in place, packs on their backs, and battle-ready weapons in their hands. Just before the command to man their vehicles, my friend Art came up to my position on the forty-millimeter antiaircraft gun to say goodbye. He first asked if I would write to him, and I assured him I would. He had already written his address on the inside of a matchbook cover and handed it to me, and I in turn reached inside my life jacket and placed it in my shirt pocket. He then handed me a roll of exposed film, pictures he had taken as we entered the battle zone, and said he would like to have a set of prints when I got them developed. With censorship, that would present a problem, but more about that later. We shook hands and said our goodbyes as he walked away to join his comrades for the assault on the beach.

From our gun station high on the port bow, we watched as these special amphibious machines and hundreds of other small landing craft moved into their assigned positions. Then on command they moved in waves toward the beach, a mass of men perhaps two hundred thousand in number. There was a constant roar of gunfire and the sound of dive bombers dropping their loads on the beach among the shattered palm trees. After the initial landings, we could view the shelling between the opposing forces as we followed the tracers arching in a rainbow across the battlefield. Then, to our amazement, we witnessed a tiny aircraft moving ever so slowly above the battlefield. It was an American spotter plane marking the positions of Japanese gun placements, which were then targeted by Navy guns and dive bombers. We all agreed the pilot of that aircraft was on hazardous duty.

As the ground forces pushed the Japanese backward into the jungle, we moved in for a landing. Once on the beach, all hands were ordered to the tank deck to unload the seventy-five-millimeter shells. We formed a human chain from the tank deck to the sand beyond the bow ramp. We were lined up side by side, all facing the same direction and taking a crate from our left and twisting to the right to pass the ammunition to the next man in line. Twisting my back severely aggravated the injury I had suffered at Navy Pier in Chicago. However, we got the ship unloaded and pulled back off the beach to an anchorage hopefully out of range of enemy shells. We then resumed our place at battle stations until nightfall. It made for a long day, but a mere inconvenience when compared to what our Army friends were going through on the beach and in the jungle.

At the close of the day, I pulled out the matchbook cover that Art had given me earlier in the day. Amazingly, he did not give me his military address but his home address back in Columbus, Ohio. Who can say why he did that, but I had no choice but to write to that address and explain that writing to him at his military address would shorten the delivery time between letters. As soon as I could, I sent a letter to the address on that matchbook cover, not knowing to whom I was writing.

In retrospect, concerning an incident I witnessed in the early days of the Leyte invasion, I wish to make a statement regarding the USS *Honolulu*, a heavy cruiser, which was torpedoed just off shore. We were not at general quarters, so those of us who were not on an assignment had the run of the ship. One of my shipmates and I were standing along the railing on the forward port side. While taking in the activities along the beach, several hundred yards away, we observed an airplane coming in over the hilltop far beyond the shoreline. It was at an elevation just above the treetops and bore down upon the shoreline. When it reached the water's edge, it dropped down, almost to the water, and released a torpedo short of the USS *Honolulu*'s port side and just cleared the ship before the torpedo tore into its target with a tremendous, explosive force and a blinding flash. The ship listed to port and was soon aided by what I recall was a destroyer, which came alongside to perhaps minimize the list. I relate this because it is what I witnessed from two hundred yards away, so close that if we had been at general quarters, my gun crew would have had the best shot at that plane. Since that day, I have read numerous accounts of this incident, but none are in line with what I saw. One account stated that the cruiser maneuvered desperately, another said the plane dodged antiaircraft fire. Not so! I am not rewriting history, I am just telling my story.

On another day in our brief time at Leyte, we were at general quarters and at anchor in a new location farther out from the beach. Shortly before dusk, we were warned of an imminent air attack. Things remained quiet until we picked up the sound of a

Japanese bomber and then spotted it approaching the anchorage area. Our gun crew sighted in on the target and notified the bridge. The word came down: "Do not fire, do not fire." We were dumbfounded but continued tracking as that plane circled, knowing the "fire" signal would soon come. The signal never came. While our attention was on that bomber, a kamikaze slammed into a nearby Australian cruiser, with great loss of life. I recall that not one shell was fired by anyone toward that plane from any ship in that vast anchorage. After GQ, we learned that the captain did not want to give away our position. Who could believe that an LST would have been chosen as a target with so many capital ships to choose from?

In less than forty-eight hours after the invasion forces hit the Leyte beach and pushed the Japanese back into the jungle, the Philippine people began coming out into the anchorage area in their outrigger canoes. They had been deprived of many things during the Japanese occupation, so they came out to trade with us things they had handcrafted for our soap, underclothing, candy, and even our sheets and pillowcases. Some had nothing to trade, so they sang for us. Two songs I recall them singing are "Pistol Packin' Mama" and "Alice Blue Gown." They were friendly and quite happy to be liberated.

On October 24, 1944, we moved in convoy out of Leyte Gulf, a date history has recorded as the day the greatest sea battle ever fought began. From all I have heard and read about that monumental engagement between the US Navy and the Japanese fleet, we had to have passed between them without even knowing it. I'm sure nobody could have predicted that such a decisive battle was just hours away, or that at its conclusion the Japanese would have been so thoroughly defeated. Other authors and historians have duly recorded the details of that battle. I only record my overwhelming gratitude for our safe passage out of Leyte that fateful day.

Resupply: New Guinea and Other Ports

Upon leaving Leyte Gulf, we headed southeast toward Hollandia, New Guinea, arriving on October 30. We were running low on supplies and fuel, and this area had become a giant supply base. Hollandia had a huge natural harbor, and it was jammed with many ships readying themselves for further assignment. We had some shore time, and it really felt good to stand on firm ground after more than three weeks aboard ship. One day while walking along the beach, I encountered a soldier doing the same thing. Typically, we ask the same questions when we meet someone new, such as "Where are you from?" We both answered, "Pennsylvania." When I mentioned my small town's name, he said his sister used to teach school there, and as it turned out, she had taught me. Small world!

There were not many civilians to be seen in that immediate area, but two I did see were walking along a road, a man and a woman. The woman was loaded down like a packhorse, the man strutting beside her carrying only a walking stick while every once in a while using it to flick a stone out of his way. It was incredible, but I guess that is the way they live on the other side of the world.

After being resupplied, we traveled to Maffin Bay, a small landing area, to take on more troops and equipment. We were beached, as opposed to being at anchor. On our first evening in that position, large shore guns, just off the bow, began firing into the jungle without warning. The shelling lasted only a short while and then ceased. When we inquired about this tactic, we were informed that the Japanese were just a few hundred yards back from the shore and it was a way to keep them at bay for the coming nightfall. It sure put a scare in us, because we had mistakenly believed New Guinea was secure.

Having loaded the ship with reinforcements, we headed back to the Philippines. We went straight to the beach where we had made our first landing on October 20. Almost as soon as the bow doors opened and the ramp hit the sandy beach, some of our Army friends from "A Day" (invasion day) came aboard to see us. My friend Art was not with them, and when I inquired about him, they told me he had been caught in crossfire and was killed. This was devastating news to me, but crushing news to whomever I wrote that letter. We had a good visit with them, and I was thankful they had survived. We remained in Leyte only long enough to unload, which meant leaving for New Guinea the following day.

We arrived back in Hollandia on November 21, 1944, where our biggest interest was mail call. As the mail was distributed, I was saddened by the imprint on the face of one letter, a letter I had written to Al Torchia, a lifelong friend, who was serving in the European theater in the US Army. The message on that letter read "missing in action." This news really set me back, for it came so soon after Art was killed at Leyte. As soon as I could, I wrote to Al's family, as they too were my dear friends, expressing my regret along with the words of encouragement. From that day on Al's mother and I exchanged letters, and it was my hope and prayer that I could lend some bit of comfort.

In that same mail, there was a letter from Art's mother in Columbus informing me that Art had been killed at Leyte. Of course, I already had that information, but in her own way she tried to break it to me gently. I answered her letter quickly and explained how on returning to Leyte I had heard the sad news from Art's Army buddies. I can't recall what all I wrote in my letter to her, for I was surely at a loss for words. Aside from my condolences, I told her a little about myself.

I always got lots of mail from Mom, Dad, Bud, and Audrey, my immediate family. Others with whom I corresponded were relatives or friends from high school. I had no girlfriend, which was a plus, as I recall the number of shipmates who got "Dear John" letters from their "true loves." My brother devised a code I could trigger by using certain words and then underlining the date if a code word was in that letter. All the code did was let him know where I was at the time I wrote it, and by the time he got my message, I would be thousands of miles away. With censorship, it was a foolish move to be straightforward in a letter about anything concerning our whereabouts or activities, so I never made any attempt to tell my parents anything. Yet time after time, they received my letters with big holes cut in them. All mail was censored by the officers, and I suppose there were days when they had a nasty streak.

During extended stays in a port where large food supplies were available, some of us would be assigned to a work party to bring supplies in our small boats. On one occasion, there was a generous supply of gallon cans of olives in our load of supplies. Since olives were one of my favorite treats, I slipped away with one of those cans and hid it until the time was right for an olive feast. Oh, how I played it over in my mind about how I was going to enjoy that feast. Knowing I could not eat the whole gallon, I invited a friend to join me in a secretive place on the ship. At the appointed hour, we met and opened the can, but to our chagrin they were black olives instead of the green, stuffed ones we had dreamed about. So as not to be caught, we slyly tossed them overboard hoping the fish could have a feast. I believe I learned another lesson: "Thou shalt not steal."

Dare I follow that confession with my concern about church attendance? Being at sea so much or in a port where no worship services were available, we were lacking something that had been a part of my life since early childhood. Most servicemen felt it their responsibility to criticize or complain about officers, and I was no different than anyone else. However, Mr. Brubaker, a schoolteacher in civilian life and a devoted Christion man, made every effort to get those of us who so desired to gather for devotions on Sunday mornings. While I had some conflicts with this man, I shall be eternally grateful for his efforts to put our minds and hearts on a higher plane amidst the tragedies of war.

Reflecting on Mr. Brubaker, I recall one day when he came through the crew's quarters and came upon a man standing in a shower stall who had two one-gallon cans full of freshwater, one for soaping down and the second to rinse off.

"What do you think you are doing? You know you are supposed to be showering with saltwater."

The man, of course, insisted he was bathing with a minimal amount of water, which he had gotten from a nearby sink. I could not help butting into the conversation.

"Mr. Brubaker," I asked, "aren't you and all the other officers taking freshwater showers up in officer country?"

"Well, ah-ah-ah . . ." His voice trailed off and he became silent.

Again I asked the question.

He owned up to what the officers were getting away with, but insisted that they were judicious in their use of water by turning it off while they soaped down. Somewhat embarrassed, he walked away.

Needless to say, nothing changed. For a time, I was assigned to the boiler room with the responsibility of maintaining hot water for the ship and to convert saltwater into freshwater. To avoid being caught with two gallons of freshwater in a shower stall, I stripped down and stood in the bilges and allowed that warm freshwater to massage my body—what luxury!

Considering the need for men and materials at the front lines, our stay in Hollandia was extensive, growing into two full weeks. This was not meant as a complaint, just an observation. We were happy to get off the ship for a few hours every other day. Also, we were getting mail almost every day, and that was a real plus. Nearing the end of our stay in Hollandia, I got a letter mailed from Glen Ellyn, Illinois. I was mystified by this postmark because I was not corresponding with anyone in that state. Upon opening that envelope, I began reading the outpouring of grief from a woman named Jean Simpson, who told me that she had been the fiancée of my friend Art and that she had been mailed the letter I had written to Mrs. Uhleman, Art's mother. There were questions she asked of me, so in response I did the best I could in answering her letter.

We finally got orders to move out of Hollandia, which is in the Dutch, northern half of New Guinea, to Finschhafen, which is in British New Guinea to the south. On this short run, Bo Sellers, one of our ship's electricians, decided to do something to get attention. He got the ship's barber to shave his head in such a way that he would have a hairline like that of a balding older man. He got attention immediately from Mr. Jones, our executive officer, who had the hairline of a balding older man. Mr. Jones was livid—he believed Bo had done this to mimic him and so ordered him back to the barber for a complete head shave. Bo became the oldest-looking teenager in our crew.

In Finschhafen, we picked up some special equipment, not a full load, and after a couple of days we headed northward to Morotai, which is in the Halmahera group of islands. As we moved in toward the beach area, we struck a coral reef and suffered a huge hole in the underside of the bow. This allowed a forward ballast tank to always be flooded, which defeated the purpose of an LST's mechanics, namely its ability to pull onto a beach and get off the beach. The principle of that forward tank, when empty, was to allow the bow to ride higher in the water, allowing it to ride up onto the beach. Once on the beach, that tank would be pumped full of water to help hold the ship in place. To ease the retraction, the tank would be pumped dry, which made it easy for the stern anchor to be used in pulling the ship off the beach. This damage severely hampered our ship in its beaching operations, but we had to cope because we were at Morotai to pick up troops and equipment for our next invasion.

It was determined that, with caution, we could meet our commitment for the coming invasion. We were at Morotai from December 18, 1944, till New Year's Day, so we had time to relax as well as load the ship. This allowed us to have a great Christmas dinner with all the trimmings, and while it was not like being home for Christmas, we knew we were having a better holiday than many of our comrades in arms.

On New Year's Day, we weighed anchor and became part of a convoy heading for the island of Luzon in the Philippines. This was a convoy that grew to more than a thousand ships before we reached our target—the beach in Lingayen Gulf.

Lingayen Invasion

During the course of our travels and through numerous mail calls, it was obvious that my dad's health was failing. He was an insurance agent for a large life-insurance company, and through the war years, there was much pressure on people in that field in the face of dwindling business, with so many off to war and fewer births. Being so far away, there was little I could do to help his cause, but I did tell him to dip into my savings if it would help him regain his health. Well, I just got word from him that we were now partners in a service station in our hometown. It was exciting news for two reasons, one being that Dad was so upbeat about this new way of life, and secondly, it assured my employment after the war. With gas rationing, there were many problems, but all was going well just the same.

The Lingayen invasion was scheduled for January 9, 1945. It was a gigantic operation, and with the huge number of ships in our convoy, it was obvious that we could not all get our men and equipment unloaded in one day, so we had to stand by and wait our turn. We spent much time at general quarters, as the Japanese had great reason to harass this operation. There were an awful lot of shells sent skyward, and what did not explode returned to earth and sea. On one occasion, we heard this loud bang within our gun station—it was not an explosion. I jumped out of my seat to see what happened, and to my amazement found an antiaircraft shell that had come straight down into our position and flattened itself on the steel deck about twenty four inches from my feet and just four inches from striking the shells that surrounded the inside of our gun position shield. What could have been a disaster proved only a reminder that a scarce number of inches separates us from this life and the next.

Another shell hit the bridge of our ship, hitting the deck between the feet of one of our radiomen. This shell exploded, causing extensive wounds to his legs and scattering shrapnel upon several other men. Having no doctor on board, first aid was rendered and then "Monty" was evacuated for further treatment. The next day he returned to our ship swathed in bandages and in good spirits. He recovered, but would carry shrapnel in his legs for the rest of his life.

Every night the Japanese would send at least one plane high over our anchorage in Lingayen Gulf. These planes had a different sound than most, and many have referred to these night raiders as "Washing Machine Charlie." Searchlights from the beach would pinpoint the plane in the sky, but our shells did not seem to harm or scare the plane away. After one fruitless encounter, we were told to cease firing while our side sent up one of our planes, a Black Widow. Shortly after, Washing Machine Charlie came tumbling down.

Along the way, I still possessed the roll of film Art had given me at the Leyte invasion. My devious mind had to work hard on a plan to send it back home. I had been accumulating various small items like coins and seashells that would fit in a plastic soap dish. I began packing this dish by first laying a "film-sized" piece of cotton at one end and filling the balance with my little items. My plan was to use some "sleight of hand" after the censoring of my package, which would cause the cotton to be replaced by the film just before the lid closed. It worked! As I looked ahead to this plot, I decided to write a letter on a narrow strip of paper and wrap it around the film. All went well and eventually the package reached home. I am not bragging about this caper, I am confessing.

After receiving word from home that the film had arrived, I "casually" mentioned in my next letter that I would like some prints made. Well, I quickly learned that nothing is "casual" to the censor. Shortly after writing that letter, I got word that the captain wanted to see me. He wanted to know something about the film that was mentioned in my letter. I found it difficult to answer him without lying, but I tried. I told him the pictures were taken by a soldier and sent to my home, and I did not even own a camera. Now those were three facts!

Mr. Jones, our executive officer, asked me to come to his office one day, which triggered some anxiety within me because I could not think of any reason for our paths to cross. He was quite friendly and said he had a job he wanted me to consider. I listened as he told me about a program the government was wanting to start. They wanted someone to write profiles of men at sea, which could be sent back to the hometown newspaper of the individual being profiled. I do not know whether this was to hype war-bond sales or for some other reason, but I agreed to give it a try. The mystery of it all was, why me? My only experience was reporting high school sport news in the local paper back home. Over a period of weeks, I managed to produce two profiles and began to realize it was taking away from my time for answering mail, so I quietly faded away from that program.

At Lingayen Gulf, we were quite fortunate to have a mail delivery within a few days after that invasion began. There was another letter from Art's mother and one from Jean Simpson, in which each thanked me for what information I could supply them through censored letters. When time permitted, I responded to both letters. This mail was a big one, and before I opened any of the letters, I glanced over the pile of envelopes to make a quick check on who had written me. One in particular caught my eye, and I laid it aside and began reading the other letters with foreboding in my heart. The letter I set aside was from Al Torchia's sister rather than his mother, whom I had been corresponding with since Al had been reported "missing in action." My only conclusion was that the family had received word of Al's death. The letter began, "Dear Red, I am writing to you because Mother is so overwhelmed with the news" — uh-oh, I knew what was coming — "that Al has been found alive and well in a German prison camp and she just isn't calm enough to write a letter, but she wanted you to have this good news." I responded quickly to that letter.

With our mission completed in Lingayen Gulf, we joined a small convoy of LSTs on January 19 and set out on a course back to Leyte, which was getting to be quite a familiar place for us. It was an uneventful voyage, and we arrived at Tacloban, the capital of Leyte, on January 23. It was nice to be in an area where there was almost no chance of air raids. Once we settled in at our assigned anchorage, it gave us time to resupply and get all the necessary preparations completed for the next invasion. In our hearts, mail call always came first. I was assigned to duty on the mail boat, which was to go ashore at Tacloban. As we waited for a berth at the post office pier, I heard someone from another boat call my name. The face was totally familiar, but I did not have the slightest idea whom I was talking to. We visited briefly, and after he gave me his ship number we parted company. After several hours of racking my brain, I realized that this person was a close buddy of Al Honsperger, the hometown friend I had gone to church with back in Boston. I then realized that Al would be on an LST anchored near our ship. Following that assumption, I had a radioman contact his ship for verification and found this to be true, so we soon got together on his ship for a visit.

Many times when we were at sea or in an area where we spent long hours at battle stations, I would grow tired and weary, so when I could slip away to my crew compartment in off hours, I would climb into my top "three-high" bunk, which was triced up at an angle. This was a no-no, but I tried it anyway, only to have the chief boatswain come charging through with a club and pound on the bunk rail and tell me to get out of there. The urge to kill came into mind every time he did that. As irritated as he made me, he became my hero when one day, as he was going through the chow line, he was dished up a heap of powdered eggs, and with those eggs in place he turned and went back through officer's country to the wardroom where the captain and some other officers were eating. There he slammed his tray down in front of the captain, who was eating fresh eggs, and demanded to know why the crew got powdered while he ate fresh. He lost that battle, but it sure took guts to challenge the captain.

My back was giving me almost continuous pain from the time we off-loaded that ammunition there in Leyte on October 20, 1944. I was sent ashore to the fleet hospital for an examination, but it proved fruitless insofar as finding a solution to my problem. Without fail, I continued to fulfill my duties, but it was getting harder to do, especially when we had to make trips to supply ships and load and unload our boat.

A Paint Job

With another invasion coming up soon, we took every opportunity to ready ourselves for what lay ahead of us. Tensions were building among the crew, but by keeping busy, time passed and we felt ready, willing, and able for our next battle. It was now February 14, Valentine's Day, and for some reason we weighed anchor and moved a few miles away to an area just offshore the island of Samar. After an overnight stay, we moved back to Leyte the following morning, only to learn our next battle had been scratched and that we were going into dry dock to have that hole in the ship's bow repaired.

Wow! What a break! No watches to stand, just rest and relaxation. Then it happened. The captain ordered all hands to report for duty "under" the ship: "You will scrape and paint the bottom of the hull to the waterline." Imagine that, a ship the length of a football field, less than a year old, needing a paint job. Paint was supplied and the work began, but at a very slow pace and a crew madder than a hornet. Then someone got the idea to thin the paint with diesel fuel, and boy did that make a difference. The captain was simply amazed at our speed, but did not realize that paint job would wash off quickly once the ship was back in the water.

All was not bad for us, because while we were in dry dock, our forces went to battle on the island of Iwo Jima. We were blessed to have missed one of the Pacific War's bloodiest, costliest battles. However, time moves on, and we were told we would leave Leyte on March 25, 1945, for a major mission deep into the heart of the Japanese empire.

Okinawa—April 1 to May 7, 1945

It was not high on tourism's list of places to visit, nor had I ever heard the name "Okinawa," but it is where we were headed. It was April 1, 1945, Easter Sunday morning, as we moved toward our landing on the beach. Before we hit land, we knew we were in a bigger battle than anything we had ever seen. The sky overhead was filled with Japanese aircraft and puffs of black smoke from exploding antiaircraft shells. It was an unbelievable sight in which we would momentarily take part. We had just secured our place on the beach and begun discharging our cargo when four Japanese planes came straight off the land in our direction, and even with all our guns blazing, we did not score a hit. Suddenly one of them peeled off and went into a steep dive right at our gun position. As I was the trainer on our 40-mm antiaircraft gun, it was my job to swing out ahead of the diving plane while the man in the pointer position calculated the height of position at which to fire. Most of our forward guns were locked in on that plane, but it never wavered while diving through a hail of bullets. I felt it would explode at any second or be the end of us, when it miraculously rolled over, missing the mast of our ship and crashing into the water forty-five feet off the ship's stern.

After that close call, the captain demanded that every effort be made to finish unloading the ship and getting her off the beach. He was rewarded by a superior effort—we were the first ship off the beach. His thought was that we could get out of that "shooting gallery" and back to a safe haven. He reported that his ship was off the beach and that he was requesting further assignment. He was given a location where our ship would drop anchor and that all the other ships coming off the beach would deposit all their fog oil and smoke pots on our ship. We would be the supply ship for such items as needed by other ships in the invasion force. This assignment lasted thirty-seven days. Things have a way of evening out. Remember how we escaped the Iwo Jima invasion?

Every day we were at general quarters (battle stations) because of constant air attacks. Those not at battle stations were on constant "fire watch" because of all the fog oil and smoke pots, which for some reason were being ignited, perhaps by shrapnel falling from the sky. All this put a heavy load on those who had to prepare food and deliver it to the many battle stations. As we neared the end of April and the beginning of May, the air attacks diminished. Tensions mounted every day to a point where best friends were at odds. We, like many, needed a little rest and relaxation.

For me, personally, I was still in constant pain from the injury I sustained in the Leyte invasion. I did not ask, but the pharmacist mate on our ship decided to send me over to a nearby hospital ship, USS *Comfort*, in an effort to get me some help. One of our ship's small boats dropped me off at the hospital ship. Instantly I felt a pang of guilt when I saw all the wounded who had been brought aboard from the battle over on the beach. However, I was ushered below deck to see a doctor. As in the past, I had the doctor's sympathy, but I did not get much pain relief. Then panic struck me as I realized the ship was moving, loaded with wounded on its way to Guam. In the midst of my distress, I was approached by an officer who asked if my name was Remaley. I answered in the affirmative, and he told me a small boat was coming alongside to take me off. I scurried down a ladder into that small boat, happy to be going back to my ship and my friends. It was not long before I became aware of how timely my "rescue" was, as soon afterward we received a message that a Japanese kamikaze plane had crashed into the USS *Comfort*. I cannot even express what I felt over hearing that message. That ship was lit up like a Christmas tree and had all the marks of a ship of mercy. Nobody had a right to dive into all those innocent people. Having been the "last man off" did not register with me until we got that tragic news. Left to my own choices, I was afraid I would cause my own departure from this world.

Being the supply ship for fog oil and smoke pots did not excuse us from producing our share of fog to cover all the ships at anchor. This was a daily chore. One evening, after laying out a cover of fog, our gun station was totally exposed—like a hole in a donut. All of a sudden, we see a plane bearing down on us at eleven o'clock, reporting same to the bridge. "Do not fire, do not fire, it's a friendly plane!" I thought it a strange thing for a "friendly" plane to be doing and would have fired at it. However, when it was directly overhead, it opened fire on a nearby ship. Imagine, if you will, who that plane would have fired on if we had fired first. Sometimes "friendly" planes can be dangerous.

Finally, on May 7, 1945, we weighed anchor and moved south out of Okinawa.

Ulithi

Oh, what a relief! Having left Okinawa behind, we set our sights on a tiny island southwest of Guam, in the Caroline Islands. As we came into port, we did not see anything to excite us, but the skies were absent of those kamikaze planes that had plagued us the past several weeks. I would have to say we welcomed being in this place called Ulithi. At least here there was peace and tranquility.

In the several days we spent at Ulithi, we were allowed to go ashore, but there was little to do for entertainment, except have a couple cans of warm beer issued to us by ship's supply. On one occasion I got so tired of standing around—there was nowhere to sit—that I looked toward a hill, where I saw several men sitting on a log. It seemed to be a good place for me to sit down. As I approached the "log sitters," I was face to face with Bill Tamburro, brother of my senior classmate, Harold Tamburro. What an unexpected surprise! We rejoiced at such a timely meeting. Of course, we talked about our little town of Verona and how good it would be to get back home.

Ulithi had more to offer than I dreamed. The days passed and we got word to move out, returning to Manus in the Admiralty Islands, the staging area for our assault on Leyte in our initial battle. Manus was just an overnight stay, so we continued our southward journey, heading for New Caledonia, a French possession to the east of Australia. We could never imagine a scarier voyage than what we encountered traveling through the Coral Sea. We came upon giant ocean swells, crossing them as opposed to rolling with them. Our ship's bow rose high out of the sea and then slammed against the water with such a force that the ship shook from bow to stern, causing the main deck to begin cracking from port to starboard. A hurried call went out to the ship fitters, who showed up with some steel plates and welding equipment. They soon had the situation under control and we were breathing a little easier. I wondered if they expected all LSTs to have this kind of trouble since there were those steel plates readily available. With this situation normalized, we then continued south toward New Caledonia.

New Caledonia

Having been in port for several days, it was decided that I should go ashore to the fleet hospital to see if someone could do something to alleviate the pain in my lower back. In due time, I was dropped off at the landing dock and found my way to the hospital grounds entrance. To my amazement, the first person I saw was Don Ricupero, a football teammate from high school. He had had a nickname as long as I had known him, "Donkey," so I shouted this in glee only to have him shout back, "Don't call me that," as we embraced in celebration. He, of course, did not want any of his friends to know his nickname. The last time I had seen Don was in boot camp in October of 1943.

I quickly learned that Don was a Navy corpsman as he asked why I was there at the hospital. Explaining my reason for being there, he said he knew just where I was to report and that he would accompany me. He stayed with me as I went through a spinal tap and some other tests, which brought me no closer to any pain relief.

After completing my session with the medics, Don told me an entertainment group was there at the hospital for rest and relaxation. The group was headed by Dennis Day, a famous Irish tenor singer. Dennis was featured on radio on *The Jack Benny Show*, a hit show at the time, just before World War II. I got the bright idea to invite this group to perform on my ship and asked Don to take me to see Dennis.

In short order, we were entering a gymnasium, and just inside we encountered Jackie Cooper, a member of the entertainment group. Up to that time, Jackie had been a famous child movie star, but in this group he was the drummer. After an introduction, I mentioned my desire for an onboard show. Jackie said that Dennis would be the one to see.

Just then, someone tapped me on the shoulder and said, "I hear you are from Pittsburgh, that's my home. My name is Tommy Riggs." Tommy was a radio personality with two voices and was known on air as "Tommy Riggs and Little Betty Lou."

Immediately thereafter another man joined in and said, "I hear you are from Pittsburgh, which is where I am from. My name is John Fritz and I play the bass fiddle in our group." It was a mystery to me how these men knew where I was from.

Lest I should forget, I must tell of another meeting that took place in my office more than thirty years later in Pittsburgh. I was telling some friends of the above meeting when a coworker butted in by asking, "What did you say about Dennis Day?" I told him about meeting this group and he replied, "My brother was in that group, he played the bass fiddle." Is this a small world, or what?

Back to the gymnasium. I said to Don that we needed to find Dennis, so we excused ourselves and soon were at the door of the man of the hour, Dennis Day. He welcomed us into his room. I quickly told him of my idea to have his group put on a show on board my ship. He immediately said it was possible if he could get clearance from regional Navy headquarters, then asked me to clear it with the captain of my ship and return the next day with an okay. After that he would get the clearance. I got the captain and Dennis together, and they set a date for an onboard show.

In the meantime, Don and I planned for a day ashore. As we neared day's end, we bumped into Dick Fitzroy, a friend and soldier from back home. Dick was overwhelmed by us meeting in a place so far from home, stating that we were the first persons from home he had met during his years of service. Then he told us that, as luck would have it, we could not get together again because the next day his outfit was going aboard ship to move northward in the Allies' advance toward control of the Pacific. The next day Dick's outfit came aboard my ship. Some things are hard to believe! He immediately asked me to find him a place to sleep. I got him a bunk in the aft sleeping quarters among about thirty Navy personnel who adopted him. He lived like a king.

The day arrived for the "show of shows." To my surprise, another troop-laden ship tied up alongside mine for the "show." I would estimate that 450 to 500 men got to see the show, all because I bumped into a buddy from back home.

Speaking of that buddy, I never saw him again. Throughout my life, things happen that amaze me. Long after the war, my son struck up a friendship with a local businessman named Dave. Yes, Dave is Don Ricupero's son, and at this writing Dave is the mayor of our small town of Verona, Pennsylvania. It is such a small world.

On to Mindanao

Having spent ten days in New Caledonia, we were enriched by a flood of mail. My mail supply was enhanced by a couple of letters from Jean Simpson, as somewhere along the way we began writing to each other on a more frequent basis, as opposed to waiting for an answer to each previous letter. I really liked this happening.

We got orders to leave New Caledonia on June 18, 1945. After leaving port we were informed that our next port of call would be, for the third time, Hollandia, New Guinea. In nine days of uneventful travel we arrived at our destination, with my friend Dick Fitzroy enjoying the cruise as a pampered soldier among a den of sailors.

You would think this story about Dick being on board *LST-1024* was to end somewhere to the north of where we were and that nothing else could add to his trip, or mine. Well, on our first day in port, while all the soldiers were in a chow line, my friend, Art Quimiro, a former high school football teammate, saw my ship and decided to pay me a visit. Art was also serving on an LST. As he walked past the chow line he saw Dick, but kept on going because he "knew" that Dick just would not be on Red's ship. On second thought, he decided to go back to the chow line to satisfy himself. Yep! Another reunion. The three of us had a grand time; in fact, we got permission to visit Art on his ship.

Following a few days' stay in Hollandia, we headed north toward the Philippines, to the largest of the islands, Mindanao. Along the way, I got into a conversation with Mr. Shelar, one of our ship's officers. I heard he was from Pennsylvania. He mentioned that he had graduated from Slippery Rock State Teachers College. When

I told him one of my high school teachers had recently graduated from that same college, he asked me his name.

"Jim Gallagher," I replied.

"He is my best friend."

He further stated that they had graduated in the same class. It amazed me to find that this officer and I had a friend in common, but this is not the end of this story.

As World War II progressed and time passed, my sister, Audrey, and brother, "Bud" (Clyde), became students at Slippery Rock State Teachers College, and who would you imagine would be among their professors? The father of this young officer on my ship! It is a small world! It is a wonderful world!

At this point I should give out some information as to why my brother, Bud, was in college rather than in the service. Bud had completed flight training toward becoming a Navy pilot when the program was discontinued. He was ushered into another Navy training program to become part of a crew manning a PT boat in the Pacific War. Having completed his training, his group was taken across the country to California by train. During that train trip, Bud came down with pneumonia, suffered an enlarged heart, and after some time in the Navy hospital was discharged. After two years at Slippery Rock, he entered dental school at the University of Pittsburgh. He spent more than fifty years as a local dentist. Audrey graduated and taught school for thirty-eight years.

We arrived at Mindanao without incident and proceeded to off-load Dick Fitzroy and all his outfit's supplies and equipment. We said our goodbyes and were thankful for all that time we shared together.

A Lull at Leyte

After our unloading at Mindanao, we traveled empty to Leyte. While there we beached to pick up supplies, cargo, and men for our next mission. With some idle time on my hands, I went topside to the bow, where I could get a good view of the activity on the beach. As I looked to my right, I saw a man walking in the direction of my ship. He walked with an unusual gait, almost as if he were limping. I recognized that walk from my days at diesel school in Chicago. It was my friend Paul Retherford, my classmate and the man who almost tore the doors off the PX back in Panama about a year ago. I yelled at him as he was passing and then hurried down to see him for ever so short a visit. Both of us serving on LSTs meant we were often in the same convoy. It was so good to see an old friend.

During this stay at Leyte, we had abundant mail. I was becoming more interested in knowing more about Jean Simpson, my pen pal from Glen Ellyn, Illinois. I learned that she was born on October 1, 1925, just eighteen days before my birthday, October 19. She told me she was a blue-eyed blonde, five feet six inches in height. I had to live with those few facts for quite some time; my imagination had to fill in the other details, but this latest mail call overwhelmed me. She sent me two full-length photos of herself. She became my "pinup girl"—what a beautiful young lady. One photo was in her Red Cross uniform, as she did volunteer work at the hospital on weekends. The second photo was of her in a nice two-piece suit. She has a twin sister who does not look at all like her; she is four inches shorter and a brunette.

We delivered our Leyte cargo of men and materials at Subic Bay, a submarine base north of Manila on the island of Luzon. It was a brief trip with the revelation of a spectacular harbor for war operations, a place I had never heard of. Now, back to Manila.

Manila

The city of Manila was won back from the Japanese after a hard-fought battle that was costly to both sides and with widespread destruction throughout the city, especially among the government buildings. We dropped anchor in Manila Bay after passing by the island fortress of Corregidor, which had been lost in a gut-wrenching battle early in the war.

We were given some shore time, and it was great to walk the streets of this famous city. Somehow, we were offered a ride by a friendly civilian in a jeep-type vehicle, but soon realized he was heading in a direction we did not choose. It was rather scary and we hollered for him to stop. We jumped out, feeling just a little safer. Having spent our allotted time ashore, we headed back to the dock to await transportation back to our ship.

As my shipmates and I waited for the "Liberty Boat," I looked over at a group of men in work dungarees and recognized one of them as Chuck Costa, president of our senior class in high school. As I was about to approach him, he turned away, and there upon the back of his shirt was printed a name with twice the number of letters in the name "Costa." It was a short-lived moment of excitement, and I turned toward my shipmates only to hear a loud voice shouting, "Remaley, what the hell are you doing here?" Yes, it was Chuck Costa. After celebrating the joy of our meeting, I asked him about the name on his shirt. He told me he had to borrow a shirt because all his were in the laundry. How close we came to not meeting each other because of a borrowed shirt.

On another day while still in Manila, Mr. Nichols of seasickness fame got the bright idea to paint the starboard engine in the main engine room.

He said, "Remaley, I want you to take four men into the main engine room and have them paint the starboard engine and the deck around it."

When we got to the engine room, I told the men to paint the deck. They pointed out that if they painted the deck, they could not get near enough to paint the engine.

"Just paint the deck," I told them.

I knew this was one of Mr. Nichols's "make work" programs, so I messed it up intentionally. When the deck was painted, we went topside, only to bump into the boss.

"How are you coming along with the painting?" he asked.

I informed him that we were all finished. He did not believe me and rushed down to see our work. He came back up like a rocket shooting flames, shouting that he wanted that engine painted. I explained to him that having four "nonpainters" paint his brand-new car with brushes would be just as senseless as painting that engine, which had a nice, factory-smooth finish. He cooled off, and that engine never did get painted, nor did I lose my stripes.

I got the feeling that Mr. Nichols did not like me. We were both redheads—that may have had something to do with the number of times we locked horns. For several months, I was in charge of the evaporator room where we converted seawater into freshwater. During each operation, there was some wait time. To pass the time, I often would remove the paint covering so many of the brass valves used in the evaporation process and then polish them. On one captain's inspections, the skipper was bug eyed when he witnessed the sparkle from the valves, but Mr. Nichols went topside and spoke to one of my coworkers, telling him that one of the saltwater-intake pipes had some "flaky" paint that Red should take care of—ever the "make work" master.

Our stay in Manila ended as we weighed anchor and moved outward into the Pacific, taking a heading northward for a second visit to Subic Bay. My dad had given me the number of a construction battalion (Sea Bees) operating in the Pacific theater, which was manned by many men from the adjoining towns of Verona and Oakmont. Upon arriving at Subic Bay, I learned that this outfit was in the vicinity, so I struck out through some jungle areas to their base of operation. After some inquiries, I was directed to a specific location where I met up with three familiar men from home: Bill Hill, a member of my home church, Roy Ayers, and Ben Tarr, who were in the gasoline business before entering the service. That reunion was a continuation of my good fortune of meeting friends from back home. My shipmates cannot get over the number of times I met someone from home, and at times I believe there was some resentment, as most of them never met anybody.

Back to Okinawa

Having fulfilled our duties in Subic Bay, we were ticketed for a return trip to Okinawa, where we had spent a hellish thirty-seven days under almost-constant air raids. Our job was to move men and materials closer to Japan until ultimate victory was achieved. Prior to the beginning of this voyage, we had received skimpy messages about some "superbombs" dropped on Hiroshima and Nagasaki, but we did not fully understand their content or their ability to wreak such havoc upon a city. They called them "atom bombs," a foreign term to us. We began to hear talk of a Japanese surrender, and just before reaching Okinawa, it became a reality: JAPAN SURRENDERED! The war was over!

This news came to us a day out from our appointed time to land at Okinawa. For the first time, we would visit this country in a peaceful setting, with memories of it representing the worst of our experiences in all our engagements. We went about the business of dispersing the men and equipment, which we brought north from the Philippines. I caused a bit of a stir when I refused to go on a work party where some heavy lifting would be involved, as my back problem kept rearing its ugly head. This did not sit well with Mr. Jones, our executive officer, and I expected to hear more from him later.

After a few days in Okinawa, one of my shipmates said he had a favor to ask of me. He asked me to compose a letter to one of his pen pals in which everything about being on board *LST-1024* was the worst thing anyone should have to endure. This was to infuriate whoever censored this letter so much that they would pass it on to the captain. His hope was to be put off the ship. I told him I would do it if he copied my writing into his own hand. He agreed, and his plan was put in place. I had put this out of my mind until the next morning, when Bernie Stadelman, the shipmate, came to me in an excited state, shouting, "It worked, it worked!"

He continued, "I'm leaving the ship immediately. The captain was really mad at me." The war was over, but they were still censoring our mail.

Well, as time passed, I related this incident to many people — not that I was proud of what I had written, but that I was a "hero" in one man's life. I played that tune to the fullest and wondered what happened to Bernie after leaving the ship. I thought he should have written to me.

About nineteen years after this incident, I was walking through a department store in Pittsburgh, Pennsylvania, when a man walked past me. For a split second, I saw the image of Bernie Stadelman in my brain and turned quickly and shouted, "Bernie," and the man turned around.

"Did you call me?" he asked.

"Are you Bernie Stadelman?" I asked, knowing that in a moment there would be some hero worship as he said yes.

"Who are you?"

"I am Red Remaley," I answered, expecting bells and whistles as he heard my name.

"Should I know you?"

"Yes, Bernie, we were in the Navy together during World War II."

He said he did not recall being with me. I tried to refresh his memory about *LST-1024* and some of the personnel, and he acknowledged being on board and knew the people I had named. I was rather stunned by what had just transpired, but knew I was about to expose him.

"How did you get off the ship?"

"I wrote a letter that angered the captain, and he kicked me off."

"Bernie, I wrote that letter."

"The hell you did, I don't even know you," he replied as he walked away. Boy, did he puncture my balloon. I guess he had told the story so often that he believed it. I now have more fun telling the whole story.

Mr. Jones and a Medical Discovery

As in most ports, Okinawa proved fruitful in providing us with mail. Over many months, I had built up quite a list of family and friends with whom I was corresponding, and enjoyed both writing and receiving letters. It was not until Jean Simpson began writing to me that mail call became more exciting as I anticipated another letter from her. I could not explain this feeling, because there had never been anything "forward" in her letters or mine. Not having a girlfriend back home allowed me to wonder if I would ever meet Jean in person. The circumstances that had initiated our writing remained a bridge to cross. Uh-oh—I had been summoned to Mr. Jones's office (executive officer).

"Remaley, I want to know why you have refused to go on any more work parties for supplies." He continued, "Do you have a physical problem or are you just f—king off?" Immediately, I knew this was not going to be a prayer meeting.

I lost my cool in that moment. "If that is your opinion of me, I will go down to my locker and supply you with letters from my parents, who are seriously concerned about my back injury that occurred during the unloading of the seventy-five-millimeter shells on the beach at Leyte."

I added, "Why would I burden them with a nonexistent injury?"

Mr. Jones interrupted me. "Remaley, I did not mean to upset you, I just wanted to get some answers."

I told him, "You could have found some answers if you would have checked on whether I was standing all my watches. I have not missed a single one."

Mr. Jones abruptly ended the meeting.

We left Okinawa, setting out for Leyte in the Philippines, which was beginning to be a favorite port of call. This was a five-day trip. We would arrive on August 29, 1945, with a one-week stay interrupted by a trip to Samar for only a day. It was during that visit to Samar that I was sent to the fleet hospital for a checkup concerning my back problem, perhaps an outgrowth of that meeting with Mr. Jones. During my hospital visit, they x-rayed my back and determined I had a fractured vertebra. While I was pleased over a positive analysis, the report did not jive with the location of the pain I was suffering in the lower-left small of my back. However, the x-ray report apparently got back to Mr. Jones, because he never bothered me again. Immediately, my engineering officer, Mr. Nichols, began a cautious approach to any job assignment he had for me, although I felt able to perform just about any task in my department.

Occupation of Japan

With the war's end, all effort was channeled into the occupation of Japan. We had not given serious thought to anything but going home, until reality set in when we began loading men, supplies, and equipment in Manila and Lingayen Gulf.

It was a few days earlier on September 2, 1945, that General Douglas MacArthur had accepted the surrender of Japan to end World War II. Here I was on board a ship loaded with some of the first occupation troops about to land on the shores of "The Land of the Rising Sun," Japan.

I approached this event with mixed emotions, none of which included being a victor visiting the vanquished. However, I had an overwhelming desire to rise early on the morning of our landing to witness the sun rising over the "land of the vanquished." With my desire fulfilled, I cannot say it gave me any special satisfaction, except to say that I had done it. In fact, I did not share this incident with any of my shipmates.

We made our landing near the city of Wakayama, dispatched the troops along with their equipment, and were standing by for our next assignment. I looked over some information my dad had sent me. He wrote me that a friend of mine from Verona, Jim Burrows, was the skipper of an LCT, a small Navy landing craft, and included its number. As I stood along the ship's railing looking out along the beach, I spotted Jim's vessel. As I hurried along the shore and approached my target, there was Jim standing on the bow and very much surprised to see me. What a wonderful reunion. What a small world!

We were in Wakayama only a couple of days but got to have liberty on one of them. As we walked the streets of this devastated city, several things stood out, one of which was the overwhelming stench of death. While I saw no dead bodies, there were pile after pile, block after block, of rubble from destroyed buildings, under which there had to be the remains of those trapped following the relentless attacks visited upon them by our Air Force. This brief look at the tragedies of war impressed upon me how blessed the citizens of the United States of America were to have fought the war on someone else's land. A second observation I made, as we wended our way through those streets, was that the streets seemed undamaged while everything else was destroyed, which led me to believe that the devastation had been caused by firebombing. A third observation, which was quite surprising, was the friendliness of the Japanese people. Perhaps their demeanor was such because they were as glad as we were that the war was over. The language barrier prevented any serious conversation.

Leaving Wakayama behind, we travelled southward for another stop at Subic Bay, with our arrival time set for October 6, 1945. The trip was uneventful, but it gave me a moment to think about Jean Simpson, as her twentieth birthday fell on October 1. She was occupying more of my thoughts as more letters flowed in each direction. I hoped for a great mail call at Subic Bay.

The day after our arrival, I was mystified by an order to go over to the hospital ship, the USS *Comfort*, which was anchored nearby. I recalled only too vividly my other time aboard that ship and my most fortunate "escape" from the tragedy of the kamikaze plane crashing into her. Upon my arrival on board, I inquired about the doctor who had treated me on that other visit. Sadly, I learned that he had been killed when that plane hit the ship. It added to my sorrow over my encounter with the USS *Comfort*. My second visit to the *Comfort* did nothing to relieve my back pain, only a word of caution, based on an x-ray, to not do any heavy lifting. I still doubted that a fractured vertebra was causing my problem, if indeed I had a fracture.

We moved out of Subic Bay, heading north along the coast to Lingayen Gulf, adding men, material, and equipment to the ship's cargo on our way back to Wakayama, Japan, with an arrival scheduled for October 21. The biggest event of that trip was my twentieth birthday on the nineteenth. How quickly I tied Jean's birthday to mine as I realized hers had occurred on a trip south from Wakayama to the Philippines, and mine on a reverse trip involving the same countries. This young lady was becoming more than a pen pal; she was disturbing my sleep. Our assignment at Wakayama completed, we returned to the Philippines to pick up another load of occupation cargo.

Our third trip to Japan was scheduled to take us to the port city of Sasebo with an arrival set for November 14, 1945. We unloaded the ship quickly and moved to an assigned anchorage. On the second day at Sasebo, we were told we were going to tie up to a Japanese submarine. When we asked where the submarine was located, a shipmate pointed to a large vessel not far from our starboard side. I tried to convince him he was in error, because a ship that size could not be a submarine. Boy, was I ever wrong!

As we pulled alongside that vessel, it made our ship look rather small, as it was said to be more than 400 feet long, compared to an LST's 327 feet. Once secured to the sub, we were allowed to go aboard and roam its inmost parts unsupervised. The sub weighed 5,900 tons, which was double the size of our Navy's subs in World War II. This sub—an I-400 class—had eight forward torpedo tubes and carried three airplanes, which could be sent aloft with the use of a catapult and be retrieved by a special derrick upon return. As we toured this mammoth ship, we learned that it was a double ship, meaning from stem to stern it had duplicates of the necessary parts to continue in battle should one side be damaged beyond control, allowing its crew to move to the undamaged quarters and continue their mission. We were in awe of this giant, top-secret weapon.

Japan had three of these subs, whose primary mission was to attack a major lock in the Panama Canal, but the war's end prevented that from happening. I referred to this giant sub as "top secret" when I later learned that the United States had scuttled these three subs to keep the Soviet Union from learning anything about their construction data. If they learned the truth, the higher-ups would have been livid to find that the crew of a lowly LST had free run of such a top-secret prize. I have no idea who authorized our tour of that sub, but it was an awesome experience.

After that exciting visit in Sasebo, anything else would have trouble measuring up to that experience. However, we just loaded up with US Marines and headed for Izuhara on Tsushima Island, which is located between the southern tip of Japan and the tip of South Korea. Our mission was to accept their surrender. As we came into port, we dropped anchor a short distance from shore as opposed to making a beach landing. Before any of the Marines could be discharged, a small boat approached the ship. As it drew alongside, a Japanese general grabbed the ladder and climbed aboard. He approached the Marine officer in charge to present his sword and was abruptly told to get off the ship and wait on shore for the "proper" surrendering. This did not sit well with those who witnessed the incident.

In due time, the surrender was accomplished on shore, and the Marines went about blowing up all the gun emplacements. The citizens of the island took to the hills out of fear of the "enemy." Gradually, they learned no harm would come to them and subsequently returned to their homes. I had the good fortune of meeting a man who could speak and understand English. He was a local schoolteacher. I learned that he had been educated in the state of California as a young man and returned to teach in his hometown. As we talked, he told me that as the war had progressed, the Japanese government had come in, rounded up all young men and boys, and taken them off to war. They had taken his son away, and he sadly related that he did not know where he was or if he was alive or not.

Addressing me, he said, "He went out to kill you, and you were out to kill him. How sad." Meeting this humble man really touched my heart.

Over a nine-day stay in Izuhara, the Marines finished their mission and came back aboard with hundreds of rifles and swords. Most everyone took advantage of the chance to get a souvenir. We weighed anchor and headed back to Sasebo, Japan, a one-day voyage, with little expectation that anything exciting would happen this time. Maybe we would at least get ashore.

Back in Sasebo, I hoped to get another glimpse of that massive sub, but it was nowhere to be seen. However, we got to go ashore, and as we saw in Wakayama, there was much devastation. As we encountered the local citizens, they were begging to buy American cigarettes, and some were rewarded by servicemen who had the foresight to bring along a few cartons. It gave the men some local cash to buy a few available souvenirs.

Liberty was not too exciting, so we headed for the landing where we would be picked up and taken back to our ship. As we waited for transportation, one of my shipmates remarked, "You finally hit a port where you didn't meet anyone!"

At that instant I was slapped harshly on my left shoulder. I turned around and was utterly shocked as I shook that person's hand. I turned to my shipmates. "I want you to meet my cousin, Art Hysong." They were floored by this encounter, as was I, for I did not know Art was in the Navy. Before leaving Sasebo, I got to visit him on his ship.

After Japan

We sensed our missions in Japan were drawing to a close as we left Sasebo and travelled to the port of Fukuoka, a day's journey, and after a few days back to Sasebo. Oh, how we wanted to go home! Well, we headed south out of Sasebo on December 22, 1945, heading to Saipan, about a week's journey. That would put us at sea for Christmas, ending our fourth trip to Japan. Our shattered dreams of being home for Christmas played heavy on our hearts in those moments of self-pity, forgetting the many fields of white crosses and stars of David in evidence all over the war zone. At least *we* would get home, eventually.

Under the circumstances, we had to make do with what we had if we wanted to celebrate Christmas. A lot of funny gifts were created, mostly for laughs, and we all, except those manning the ship, gathered in our empty tank deck and sang a lot of Christmas carols. Somehow, I got conned into dressing as Santa, but my suit, which was supposed to be red, was a dungaree blue trimmed in white cotton. A black-and-white photo would not reveal this shortcoming. Oh well, I said we had to make do with what we had. We arrived on time at Saipan and stayed there for two weeks, just killing time. We wanted to go home! A one-day trip took us to Guam.

We felt like a game of sorts was going on, because we began loading up for a return trip to Saipan. Meanwhile, as I was involved in a project, I heard someone call my name and turned to face two men from Verona, Ron Hopkins and Bill Phillips. That increased the unimaginable number of people I met from home.

Meeting Ron reminded me of one of the most regrettable things I had ever done. Bear with me, this will take a little explaining. Between high school graduation and my entrance into the military services, I worked for a furniture company. One day a young girl I had met before came into the store with her mother. She immediately struck up a conversation with me about her mother's "new car" (used). She insisted I go outside and see it. There at the curb was a 1941 Packard convertible, two-tone green with white sidewall tires, spares mounted in each front fender and glistening in the sun. You would have had to live in that era to appreciate what I was looking at.

"What do you think of Mom's car?" she asked.

What a silly question, I thought, but answered, "I would like to go for a ride in it."

We returned to the store and she said to her mother, "Red would like to go for a ride in your car." Her mother said it could be arranged. A few days later Betty got in touch with me and said she got permission to have Mom's car on Saturday evening. The arrangements were made to meet me in front of the family pharmacy on the main street in Verona and to bring a friend. That friend was Ron Hopkins. Betty would bring a friend also. As in most small towns, on a Saturday evening, there would be a number of guys watching all the girls go by the pharmacy. These "oglers" were our friends and wanted to know why Ron and I were so dressed up. We told them a couple of girls would be picking us up in a convertible in a few minutes. They jumped on us about being such big liars. Momentarily a beautiful Packard convertible pulled up to the curb, and Ron and I climbed in and drove away without saying another word, to the oglers' chagrin.

Betty drove us through several communities, one of which was Blawnox, a small town on the opposite side of the Allegheny River. I asked her if she would let me drive, and she answered in the affirmative. We changed places in the front seat.

I drove slowly out of Blawnox, and feeling a little big for my britches, I asked, "Will this car do a hundred miles per hour?"

She did not know. I put the pedal to the floor—fifty, sixty, seventy, eighty, ninety, and then ninety-seven. In that moment, guilt struck a chord in my brain, making me feel so stupid that I took my foot off that pedal upon realizing how close I may have come to ending all our lives. Never, never in my life did I ever put the pedal to the floor again. The regret of what I did that Saturday evening has never left me, nor the betrayal of a mother's daughter who was trusted with a trophy car. I pray that this incident will prevent even one person from "putting the pedal to the floor." I suspect that my Silent Partner had something to do with me not reaching that one hundred miles per hour.

Back to my visitors, I told them we were going back to Saipan. I hated the thought of returning to a place where so much tragedy had taken place place during its recapture, things I had not mentioned on our initial visit. The citizens of Saipan had panicked, or were misled by propaganda, or whatever, and had rushed to the highest cliffs and jumped to their deaths by the hundreds. Some women had thrown their children off the cliff before jumping themselves, others had jumped while holding infants in their arms. The unthinkable had been repeated over and over again, and I doubt anyone will ever know the numbers involved in that horrible tragedy.

The Separation

I was not ready for this! I had been summoned by the head pharmacist's mate and told to pack my gear for transfer to Fleet Hospital 103 on Guam. What a traumatic moment this was for me, as I would be leaving all my friends with whom I had shared so much—immediately! It was the twenty-fifth of January 1946. This ship had been my home since May 28, 1944. I would not have time to say goodbye to more than a few of my shipmates.

I had packed my sea bag, including two Japanese swords, but did not have enough room for the rest of my belongings. I was saved by Larry Smiraldi, a shipfitter, who had fashioned a suitcase out of his scrap pile and sold it to me for five dollars. This was all for my own well-being, but I was saddened by it all, as I would never again see most of the men I was leaving behind.

As the hospital bus pulled away from the dock, I at least had the satisfaction that I wouldn't have to make that trip to Saipan. There was not much solace in that, for what lay ahead could be more dismaying. In our stay in Guam, I had been blessed to have received a lot of mail from all my friends, relatives, and Jean. This young lady was occupying more and more of my thoughts— would I ever meet her? What would result from such a meeting? Having a new address would reduce my incoming mail, because it would all follow *LST-1024*, eventually reaching me, unless I was on a hospital ship heading for the States.

Upon arriving at the hospital, I was assigned a bed in a huge ward filled with lots of strangers. In time, I made a few acquaintances, which likely would not equal the closeness I had with my shipmates.

One day I met another man, who turned out to be a blessing, for we hit it off from the beginning. His name was Ted Musial, whose home was in the Polish section of Detroit, Michigan.

There was not much going on at the hospital, but one night, a Marine in the bed next to mine began screaming. He had had knee surgery that day, and in the wee (no pun intended) hours of the morning, he could not pass his water. I got a nurse to come to his aid and assisted her in putting a catheter in the patient. I can hardly believe how much water came out of that man.

The days passed slowly. In fact, Ted and I counted in weeks—we were in the middle of the third week at the hospital. A loaded hospital ship left today bound for the States, and we were sorry we were not on it. An activity, arranged by the Red Cross, took us on a bus tour of Guam that afternoon. It was a great change of pace, and we got a view of Guam we would not have gotten otherwise. We were told there were still many Japanese soldiers in the jungles of Guam, because they refused to believe the war was over, that their nation would surrender. We enjoyed the trip, and along with beautiful scenery, it proved to be informative.

The boredom of our stay was broken last evening as we got to see a live stage show featuring Thomas Mitchell. The only other live entertainment I got to see overseas was the show aboard *LST-1024* with Dennis Day, Jackie Cooper, and others. I deeply appreciated the efforts of these notable personalities in boosting the morale of those in the service of our nation.

Wow! What a day! I think I shed a few tears. Resting near my bed, I looked up as footsteps approached. There to my amazement were Jack Felger and "Griff" Griffin, two of my best friends and shipmates from *LST-1024*. They had returned from Saipan and took a chance that I might still be in this hospital. It would be impossible for me to describe the joy these men brought to my heart, for I never expected anyone to visit me. After rejoicing over this reunion, I asked Jack and Griff to follow me. I led them into the kitchen, got two glasses, and poured out some milk, the first fresh milk for them since they had left the States. Griff had a peach-fuzz mustache full of milk. What a joy! They informed me that the ship was reloading for another trip back to Saipan on February 23. I had been there for nearly a month. When another hospital ship sailed out and I was not on board, I was really upset and took my case to the doctor in charge. I asked why I had been passed over for transit to the States. He said I had refused to swab the deck in my ward. First of all, I had never been asked to swab anything, and good grief, why would a patient with back trouble be expected to perform such a task? I informed him that most any task would have been a relief from the boredom of doing nothing. Subsequently, I became the mailman for several wards.

Speaking of mail, much of my personal mail caught up to me when *LST-1024* came back to Guam. There were letters from most of my friends and relatives, and two from Jean. Sadly, she informed me that her Great-Uncle Will, who had lived with her family all her life, had passed away. When Art Uhleman had been killed in the Leyte invasion, Uncle Will had lamented that an old man like himself should have died instead. Within a period of less than eighteen months, Jean had lost two people who meant very much to her.

Through my writings, I have expressed different feelings about this relationship with Jean. First, she was controlling my thoughts more and more, and she was disturbing my sleep. I wondered if I would ever meet her, and if we did meet, what would be the result. Was I in love with a person I had never met? I had not discussed my feelings with anyone, but I had strong feelings that this could be happening, you know, like in the movies. As I said before, it was still a bridge to cross.

Homeward Bound

This morning we awoke to the greatest news since Japan's surrender: WE WERE GOING HOME! The hospital ship USS *Hope* was in the harbor here at Guam. Praise God! We gathered our gear to make that final voyage to the land of the free and the home of the brave. We were all so hyped up that we thought we could walk on water, but seriously, we better take the ship called *HOPE*.

It took many bus trips from the hospital to the ship with possibly seven hundred patients, many on stretchers or wheelchairs, but we were all here. Look out America, here we come! We were in a spacious ward, with much room to walk around in. We anxiously awaited the sound of churning propellers and a refreshing sea breeze.

We were now two days out from Guam on a beautiful, calm sea. Things had not been completely calm, however, as those of us who were mobile lined up for noon chow. We were all dressed in full-length bathrobes and had a rather sameness about our appearance. All was calm in the chow line. Ted was in front of me. Without warning, a guy walked up alongside us and squeezed in ahead of Ted. This upset Ted very much, and he shouted at the man to get at the end of the line or he would throw his ass overboard. The bully who broke into the line never said a word and remained in place while Ted kept chattering about his brazenness. The line moved and we all ate well and returned to our ward. Shortly, another patient approached Ted and told him not to endanger his well-being by challenging that bully in the chow line, because he happened to be Mr. Michigan, champion weight lifter. *Gulp.*

Ted remained calm and became inquisitive about Mr. Michigan. He learned that he was Polish, like Ted, and that he also lived in Hamtramck, the Polish section of the city of Detroit. They were practically neighbors! Ted softened and said he wanted to meet this "weight lifter," so we went with this informant and he introduced us. I stood there as these two Polish adversaries gushed all over each other as they compared notes about their hometown. This outcome, after the tiff in the chow line, was unbelievable. We became a trio, spending most of the voyage together, and simply called Mr. Michigan "Ski."

The balance of our homeward voyage was most enjoyable. We ate well and had beautiful weather and calm seas. At night, before lights out, we waged cigarette battles. All of us received a carton of cigarettes at boarding. Apparently there were very few smokers, as we emptied those cartons by whaling single packs at anyone in the ward within reach of our arm strength. In the morning, the deck was covered with cigarette packs, which we scooped up for the next night's battle.

"There it is, there it is!" we heard someone shout. It was the Golden Gate Bridge off in the distance. It is not unusual for that bridge to be shrouded in fog, and this day was no exception, but as we came closer to the coast, the image of the bridge became sharper. From that first sighting, until we got close to the bridge, it seemed like an eternity. Just as we neared the bridge, a huge pontoon vessel came out from under it to greet us and welcome us home with a band playing patriotic music. There were many tears shed during those moments. We were home at last!

As we moved under the Golden Gate Bridge, I thought about my leaving New York Harbor and the Statue of Liberty on my way to war—what a charmed circle on my journey. As the USS *Hope* made a turn to the starboard, Alcatraz came into view off our port side, a thrill for those of us who had never seen this famous rock.

We were soon docked in San Francisco, methodically removed from the ship, and transported to Oak Knoll Naval Hospital while our gear was being unloaded. What joy to set foot on the soil of the good old USA!

In my introduction to this book, I stated that "there have been times when I walked with God and times when I did not, but through it all He never deserted me." As you have read, in these pages, some different incidents might have resulted in my demise, but by God's grace I am safely back in the States, a hope fulfilled. It is ironic that my final voyage was achieved on a ship called *Hope*. I gave God the glory and my everlasting praise for my life's journey thus far, and I trusted in him for my future, as I soon would don the clothes of a civilian.

Home at Last

I managed to get to a telephone in the service center here at Oak Knoll and got through to Mom and Dad. What a joy after all these months. I am sure they breathed a sigh of relief to know of my safe return, and I was supremely grateful to hear their voices. Jean had sent me her phone number, so I put through a call to her and was happy that she was the one to answer my call. It was a joyful experience, but we both seemed at a loss for words. I told her I would call again. I had not had any mail for a long time and doubt that any will catch up to me any time soon, nor have I taken time to do any writing.

On my second day at Oak Knoll, I went to a storage area to get my sea bag. I had kept my "five-dollar suitcase" with me on our voyage from Guam. When I was presented my sea bag, I found it dripping wet, totally soaked. I asked what had happened to it and was told that in the process of unloading it from the ship, the cargo net had broken and my belongings and those of many others had dropped into San Francisco Bay. There was such a stench to all my things except for those two Japanese swords, which were the only things I could save. There I was with only a few clothes, which were in my suitcase. I had no dress uniform and almost none of the essential clothing. I quickly bought all-new clothes and had a tailor make me a new set of dress blues. I had to fill out a form, which was, in effect, a suit against the government for my loss. This was not the beginning I expected.

Ski was off doing his own thing, so Ted and I decided to take a trip up to Sacramento to visit my dad's sister, Iva, and her husband,

Jack, and their family. They had lived in Oil City, Pennsylvania, until just after the beginning of World War II when they moved west. It was early in the day, so we decided to hitchhike to Sacramento. It did not take long to get our first ride with two young men in a '38 Ford. I do not know whether that car had a souped-up engine, but they were going so fast that Ted and I were pushed hard against the back seat. How fast they were going I do not know, but I began thinking about that ride I had in a Packard convertible and the danger I had placed in the lives of four people. I decided we should bail out and told those men to let us out. Our first car ride was unforgettable. Eventually, we arrived at Aunt Iva's and were warmly received. I especially enjoyed getting reacquainted with my cousins. We stayed overnight and returned to Oak Knoll the next day by bus.

The following week, Ted and I decided to go back to Sacramento, as Uncle Jack asked me to get him some underclothes such as the ones I had to purchase in Navy supply. This time we decided to take the bus in order to avoid another "speed" incident. It was a little early for the bus, so we had two beers while waiting. One good thing: it was an express, nonstop trip. Halfway to Sacramento, Ted and I needed a pit stop to get rid of our beer. I approached the driver and explained our problem, and he quickly reminded me that we were on a nonstop express bus. I pleaded with him to make a stop, and after a bit of pondering, he said that up ahead in a small town there was a gas station where he could pull off the road. There he would let us off for a potty stop. He told us if we were not back on board in two minutes, the bus would be gone. I do not believe any other gobs could have beaten our time. We came flying back to the bus panting, taking our seats—to the roar of laughter from all the other passengers. Lesson: do not drink beer before taking the express bus.

After another good visit with my relatives, we boarded a bus late at night and headed back to Oakland. We were almost into Oakland when I awoke and discovered that Ted was not in the seat beside me. I looked throughout the bus and did not find him.

I then talked to the bus driver about Ted, and he told me that after a stop in Vallejo, he had been one passenger short.

Well, what could have happened to Ted? Did he get mugged, and was lying somewhere in need of help? Many things went through my mind during those miles into the bus depot. I was quite worried about my friend and looked throughout the bus depot hoping to find him. This delayed my return to the hospital, and I wondered what I should say in reporting his absence. Hurrying to our ward to sign in, there was Ted sitting on his bed, laughing at me and my tardiness. After missing the bus in Vallejo, someone had picked him up and driven him straight to the hospital. By this time, and after all that had happened on our trips to Sacramento, we decided not to go again.

The authorities began polling the patients, asking what hospital they wished to be sent to for final treatment. It was easy for me to choose Great Lakes Naval Hospital near Chicago, Illinois, because it was only forty-three miles from Glen Ellyn, Illinois, where Jean lived. Once I was assigned that hospital, I called Jean to let her know I was coming soon.

On to Illinois

It took a convoy of buses to get us all to the railroad station where we would soon depart for Great Lakes Naval Hospital. This was a special train, made up as a mobile hospital with special dining cars for our meals. One would call it luxurious, for we wanted for nothing. We were not moving fast, but we were in motion almost twenty-four hours a day for more than two days, sometimes waiting on sidings for scheduled trains to pass. It was an uneventful trip with Ted, Ski, and myself making up a trio. We enjoyed some beautiful scenery crossing the mountains and eventually reached Great Lakes on April 6, 1946.

After being billeted in a ward at the hospital along with our belongings, I was anxious to call Jean to let her know I had arrived. I got through to her, and she said she would visit me midafternoon of that day. Fortunately, it was a Saturday and she did not have to work. I was on pins and needles until she arrived.

I knew in my heart that I was in love with Jean, and had been for quite some time. The door opened and in walked the most beautiful girl in the world, no prejudice here, with her mother. I walked toward her, put my arms around her, and kissed her on her lips and felt her kissing me back. What a glorious moment! I confess thinking that I had been prepared for this moment, but I felt like I was botching it. After meeting her mother and exchanging pleasantries, she left Jean and me together and went for a walk. Jean and I walked outside and found a convenient park bench to sit on. We talked, but the conversation did not seem to relate to our new situation, a relationship I had anticipated for so many months.

walked around through the museum and talked excitedly as we compared notes about the happiness in our lives. My family took note that I was walking with a limp, which had appeared after my back injury at the Leyte invasion.

My family was rather exhausted after their long journey from Pennsylvania, so it was good that I had reserved two rooms at the Stevens Hotel, where we all took refuge. It was great getting reacquainted with family, but soon we all had the urge to turn in for the night.

Morning came too soon. We ate at the hotel, looked around at some of the city, which was somewhat familiar to me as I had taken my diesel training here at Navy Pier in 1943. Soon it was time to head westward to Glen Ellyn and a meeting of families. Only Bud knew how I felt about Jean; the others had not considered what was happening between me and my pen pal.

We arrived at the Simpson home with little fanfare, just a happy meeting of two families. It was not long before we were seated together in the dining room enjoying a wonderful meal and getting to know each other. My family's plan was to leave as early as possible and head back to Pennsylvania, which rather dominated the conversation—the distance would be over five hundred miles. I was glad our families got to meet each other, because I wanted my family to meet my future wife, and for the Simpsons to meet the family in Jean's future. As the Remaleys were ready to leave, I informed my mother that I was going to marry Jean, though I had not discussed that with Jean. I sensed Mom was not warm to the idea. Perhaps my having been away for so long had something to do with it, and she was not ready to share me.

Early in the evening, Jean's parents went next door to visit the Selkes, and sisters Jane and Laura disappeared. It looked like a planned evacuation. However, it was much appreciated, as Jean and I had not had any serious time together since the day we first met. We sat on the living room sofa expressing our feelings for each other and what the future had in store for us. I proposed marriage and she said yes, then I reached into my pocket and pulled out a diamond engagement ring and placed it on her finger, a ring I had just happened to purchase at the hospital gift shop during the week. Of course, we sealed it with a kiss, then sat there wondering what her mom and dad would have to say. After all, we had just met eight days ago and had not yet had our first date.

We were overjoyed at our engagement and decided to go next door and break the news to parents and neighbors. There was shock, stunned silence—then congratulations, hugs, and kisses. Jean's dad was a quiet man who was slow to rise or speak. I watched him closely as he moved toward me. He reached out, shook my hand, and congratulated me—wow! What a relief! It was a little early, but I began calling Jean's parents Mom and Dad. It sure seemed more comfortable than Mr. and Mrs.

The morning after our engagement, we took Jean to the train station. I wanted so much to stay with her, but was due back at the hospital. One thing that was special about kissing her goodbye was that she was my fiancée, not just girlfriend. Mom was so good about driving me to and from the hospital, where not much was happening in regard to my condition or what would be the disposition of my case. I had not been home since leaving New York on my way to war in the Pacific theater. I thought perhaps I could get a weekend pass for Easter, which was the next weekend. Back at the hospital, I was able to get that needed pass.

Going Home

I got away from the hospital early enough on Friday to meet Jean in Chicago after her workday, meeting Ed, the conductor, who gave me another voided ticket before boarding the train. I was taking Jean home with me, so she had a full evening of packing ahead of her, for we would be taking a night train out of Chicago on our way to Pittsburgh. Mom and Jane took us into Chicago Friday evening to get this train. At this time, trains were steam driven, crowded, and dirty. Somehow, soot would get all over your clothes, and after a few hours your face needed to be washed. I did not let that bother me, as I was able to hold Jean's hand while we slept away part of our trip—what a joy. The train was so crowded that some people did not have a seat and sat on their luggage in the aisle.

By and by our train pulled into Pittsburgh, and we were met by brother Bud and driven out to Verona. Jean was somewhat disappointed at the terrain in this area, as she had envisioned high mountains instead of hills. However, as we entered the house, there was a fully decorated Christmas tree in the living room. This was Easter weekend in April. Who could imagine something more surprising than having someone save that tree for your homecoming? I had a feeling the tree represented a vigil experienced by many who had sort of kept a "light on" for that expected loved one coming home from the war. It was a sight I shall never forget.

Home at last, home at last, how I had dreamed and prayed for this moment to come. The house was not really home to me, as my parents had purchased it just a few months before I joined the

Navy, but it was home in a real sense because it was the gathering place of our family. Take away family and you have no home. We all rejoiced in these first hours together, and I deeply prayed for Jean's acceptance as family, because she would be leaving her roots and family after our marriage, as we would take up residence in Pennsylvania. That is a great sacrifice for one who has never been away from home.

This was a two-bedroom house with only Mom and Dad normally in residence. Now two college students were on Easter vacation, plus Jean and myself, but somehow we all found a place to sleep, with Jean and Audrey sharing one of those bedrooms.

We awoke to a beautiful Easter morning, a day of peace and quiet, filled with the joy of being together. It was not hard for me to recall where I had been on Easter morning a year ago—aboard the *LST-1024* on the beach at Okinawa under attack by Japanese kamikazes. As described earlier, it was by the grace of God we survived that day—and others that followed. How great is the dawn of a new day in a world at peace.

Jean and I attended the church of my childhood, where we were greeted by so many friends I had not seen in several years, among whom was Jim Beers, one of my high school classmates, like me still in his Navy dress blues. I had many fond memories of the Verona Methodist Church and those who had taken the time and preparation to teach me in Sunday school up to the age seventeen, when I joined the Navy. It was good to be back.

The Coming Wedding

Following the wonderful Easter weekend in Pennsylvania, Jean and I returned to Illinois. Jean to her job, and me back in the hospital. On Wednesday, April 24, I was scheduled for an evaluation exam. Earlier, in the hospital on Samar, in the Philippines, they had determined that I had a fractured vertebra, which seemed too far from the point of my pain. The x-rays here at Great Lakes Naval Hospital proved I did not have a fracture, but neither did they prove that some other problem existed. As the physical exam continued, it was determined that my right leg was three quarters of an inch shorter than my left leg, which explained why I had had this limp since my injury.

Well, what now? I had had no relief from my pain, and no doctor or test had given me any satisfaction as to what was at the root of my problem. Nobody doubted I was in pain. The doctor here had recommended that I have all my shoes altered to offset the shortness in my right leg. He was apologetic in not solving my problem and recommended me for discharge from the Navy. Further, he advised me to fill out disability forms at the discharge center so there would be a permanent record of my case should there be further pursuit concerning my problem. I was scheduled to go to the process center at Great Lakes on May 1, where I would be discharged.

Meanwhile, I had a weekend pass to go to Glen Ellyn and be with Jean. I was looking forward to my discharge so we could be together before my return to Pennsylvania. The plan was for Jean's mother to pick me up on Friday, April 26, at the hospital's main gate. As I waited at this gate by the highway, I looked to my left, and far down the road I could see a sailor walking away. He had an unusual way of walking, reminding me of my friend Paul. I had nothing to lose, so I shouted at the top of my voice, "Hey Retherford!" The sailor turned around and came back up the highway—it was my friend Paul. Chance had given us one last reunion. What a small world. Paul had just been discharged and was heading home.

The weekend with Jean was truly wonderful, as I was happy to be with her, but it also gave me an opportunity to get better acquainted with her family. We did some serious talking about setting a wedding date. We chose September 14, 1946, just five months from the day of our engagement on April 14. Many thought we were rushing it, but Jean and I were not among them. We were so in love. Following my discharge during the week, we would get deeper into our wedding plans.

On May 1, I went to the process center for discharge, only to be informed that I would not be discharged at Great Lakes. To my amazement, they were sending me to Bainbridge, Maryland. I was really upset over this turn of events, and I argued strongly for a local discharge, to no avail. They gave me a railroad ticket to Bainbridge with some delayed orders that allowed me to stop in my hometown on the way. I had to gather my belongings and make some quick goodbyes to Ted and Ski, who were continuing to cement their friendship.

After a couple of days in Verona with my parents, I went on to Maryland. They offered me another stripe if I would sign over for another hitch. I was a second-class motor machinist's mate, and all I wanted was out. I signed those papers suggested by the doctor, and when asked where I wanted transportation to, I quickly said, "Back to Chicago." The government at work. Since I had entered the Navy at Great Lakes, it seemed logical to discharge me there.

I took the ticket and practically ran toward the gate out of fear that somehow my discharge would be voided. Outside the gate, I felt a freedom that was just indescribable. For me, at that moment, the war was truly over. I quickly made it into Baltimore, where I caught a train to Pittsburgh and then home to Verona. This was May 6, 1946, my first time out of uniform since I had joined the Navy in September 1943. I must admit it felt awkward not being under the thumb of some military authority, but I soon learned to get used to it. Those first few days were spent getting reacquainted with "things civilian." Civilian clothes were a first order of business, because the only garments waiting for me were the things I had worn in high school.

Spending time with Dad at the gas station was a priority, since that was where I expected to earn a living. However, I listlessly went through the motions on the job, because my heart was with Jean way out there in Glen Ellyn, Illinois.

In addition to wanting to go back to see Jean, I had a promise to fulfill in visiting Art's family, the Uhlemans. Believe me, I did not relish making that visit. The days of my first week as a civilian passed, and the weekend brought our family of five together, with Bud and Audrey home from college. Sunday we were to take them back to school by way of my grandmother's farm over in Ohio, recalling that Granddad had died while I was overseas. This farm was only two miles from the town of Petersburg, Ohio. In my earlier writings, I explained how Jack Felger, from New Springfield, Ohio, had come into the crew of *LST-1024* and that he knew my relatives on this farm. Well, Jack's sweetheart lived in Petersburg; her name was Mamie.

Jack was one of my closest friends among all my shipmates. The last time I saw him was in the fleet hospital in Guam when he and "Griff" Griffin had paid me a visit. I had lost contact with him, but remembered him saying Mamie lived along the main road that passed through the town of Petersburg. I felt the loss of those friendships that had developed over those months aboard ship. Through Mamie I hoped to learn something as to where Jack was, in service or out.

As we left the farm, I asked Dad to drive over to Petersburg so I could look up Mamie in order to get in touch with Jack. Dad assumed I had her address, so he drove over to that little town. I remembered a picture Jack had of Mamie standing under a willow tree in her backyard. Dad asked where she lived. I said I did not have an address, but just drive down the main road and look for a willow tree in the backyard. That went over like a lead balloon. Dad was furious. However, as we drove along Main Street, I spotted a willow tree on the left side and shouted to Dad to pull in that driveway. Reluctantly, he obliged.

I got out of the car, went to the back door, and knocked. The knock was answered by a young woman with half of her hair up in curlers and the rest in disarray.

I asked, "Are you Mamie?"

She said, "Yes."

I got all the information I needed about Jack and returned to the car, from which I had heard several toots of the horn during my visit. There was total silence, but inwardly I was doing a belly laugh. It pays to know your trees. In spite of this strange encounter, Mamie and Jack became lifelong friends with my parents and with Jean and myself. It's a wonderful world.

Monday morning began with Dad and me at the gas station, which was gradually becoming more comfortable for me as I learned some of the techniques of doing a grease job and fixing flats or mounting new tires. Everybody expected you to check their oil level, so it was important to learn which side of the engine had the dipstick. I enjoyed meeting the customers who had become Dad's regulars. Dad and I got along well, but as I talked frequently about my plans to visit Jean, he became rather testy, for my absence would require the hiring of a substitute. I understood his concern, but proceeded to set a date for going away. I expected to be gone a week to ten days, along with fulfilling that promise to visit the Uhlemans, who lived in Columbus, Ohio.

I managed to get off to Illinois by train to Chicago and then to Glen Ellyn by local electric train. Jean had time off, so we did a number of things together. We had our first date at an amusement park with one of Jean's friends, Jackie, and her boyfriend. Jean's dad was a grain broker on the Chicago Board of Trade, so she took me there to watch how they did trades in the pits. It was quite interesting to watch the exciting action as the traders used special hand signals to make their trades. I learned that you could lose your shirt in that business if the markets dipped unexpectedly.

On another occasion, Jean took me to her office in downtown Chicago where she worked as a keypunch operator and secretary. She introduced me to her coworkers, and among those workers was a couple who had special feelings for Jean, the boss and his wife, who were secretly married and became our lifelong friends. Their names were Florence and Phil Gherke. We met Jean's dad for lunch and then headed home. I was so happy being with her.

Some evenings were spent with Jean's parents taking us to visit their longtime friends who wanted to meet this young man who had come on so strongly to their friends' daughter. I enjoyed meeting these people along with relatives. Too soon time was running out, and we had to part until another day. How sad was the parting. I was weighed down by that visit to Art's family, and just wished it would be over with.

The date was set, so the Uhlemans knew I was coming. The meeting had to be in God's scheme of things all the way back to October 20, 1944, when Art had come to my battle station and handed me that matchbook cover with his home address on it. Why had he done that? Only Art and God know why, but from that moment until now I have been at the heart of something stranger than fiction. I wrote one letter and got two in return: one from Mrs. Uhleman and one from Jean Simpson, Art's fiancée. Mrs. Uhleman had written to tell me of Art being killed in the battle for Leyte, but had not informed me that she had passed my letter on to someone else. This second letter followed the first by just a few days and was, of course, from a grieving young lady. I would never have come to know Jean had it not been for Mrs. Uhleman. How else could two people so widely separated in this world have become so deeply and dearly attracted to each other? I knew that one day I would knock on the door of Art's home, but only in the wildest of dreams could I be engaged to his fiancée when that moment approached. The weight of this situation had been frightening. As

I have written, I corresponded with these two ladies for the better part of a year and a half, a time that dramatically affected my life.

I knocked on the door. As the door opened, my feet felt as though they were weighed down with lead, not wanting to take the next step.

"Come in," a voice said. "I am Art's mother."

I moved cautiously into the Uhleman's living room and quickly took note of a beautiful studio photograph of Art and Jean there upon the wall. It did not trouble me; after all, they had had special plans in their lives. I was introduced to Mr. Uhleman, sister Kate, and "Goldie," a friend of the family whom Jean had mentioned on several occasions. Through a bit of small talk, I learned that one other person, who had been with Art during the war, had visited the Uhlemans. His name was Lou Groza, who became well known as "Lou the Toe," as he became the field goal kicker for the Cleveland Browns, the NFL football team. He had been in Art's Army division, and had likely been aboard *LST-1024* at Leyte. As attempts were made to make me comfortable, I was very uncomfortable. They knew I had strong feelings for Jean, and right or wrong, I did not mention our engagement.

I dreaded what might be coming during this visit. Suddenly, Mrs. Uhleman said, "I have one question to ask of you." *Uh-oh, what am I in for?* "Was Art afraid?" she asked. I was so unprepared for such a question. How could one man answer such an inquiry of another man?

For a moment, I felt up against a wall, but mustered the courage to say, "No."

Then I felt a need to recall Art's demeanor as he had talked to me and the members of my gun crew. As we had talked over the noise of the bombardment at the nearby beach, we had all been in a jovial mood. Remember, this was the first battle for all of us, and I had not detected any fear in Art, only a boldness about the battle. I answered one question. Did I do Art justice? Only God knows.

The Uhleman visit was now history, and returning home was more welcome than I could imagine, as that burden was now lifted.

In my mail, I received a letter from the US government informing me that I had been awarded a 10 percent disability rating, which qualified me to receive monthly $11.50. I was pleased for the quick decision on my case. At least it left the door open to further treatment should someone determine what was causing my pain.

Just a few days after arriving home Dad, Bud, and I were involved in a maintenance project when a car pulled alongside the curb. The passenger window was down and there was a beautiful young lady waving to us. I could not imagine who she was until the driver got out and walked around the car. The driver was Jack Felger, and the beautiful lady was the young girl I had seen in a snapshot many months ago standing under a willow tree in her backyard in Petersburg, Ohio. Mamie stepped out of the car. She sure did not resemble the young person with half of her hair up in curlers whom I had met a few weeks before. What a wonderful moment for Jack and me, reunited in friendship from that day on for life. A joyous reunion! Along with Mamie and Jack were his parents, Helen and Fred. After the introductions were made, we settled in the house for a wonderful get-acquainted session. I wondered, at the moment, if Bud and Dad thought about a willow tree in Petersburg, Ohio. How remarkable to have met Mamie because of that tree.

Having had a couple of months in civilian life, I began meeting my prewar friends in the Verona's shopping district in the evening. None of us had a car, so we did a lot of walking. Some had jobs, some did not. Of course, I had a job with Dad at the station. In the rough, we called it a gas station, but in those days it was really a service station, because people came in expecting the works. Customers came in, basically for gasoline at 17.9 cents per gallon, but expected an oil-level check, tire-pressure check, water-level report, and front and back windows cleaned. They could drive away after spending a buck for more than five gallons of gasoline. This was 1946, and we prided ourselves on giving service. Somehow, that word is lost at today's gas stations.

Dad was a good mechanic when it came to working on cars, and was not afraid to tackle any job on his own automobile. He was not interested in making a living as a mechanic. In early July of 1946, Dad was doing some major repair work on his car's engine, so we had to walk to and from work for a couple of days. The station was just over a mile from home. One of those days, as we walked to work, I spotted a folded bill on the sidewalk. As I retrieved it, I expected it to be a dollar bill, but was overwhelmed to discover number tens on each corner. Wow, what a lucky day! Dad teased me by saying, "You should have let me pick it up." We walked about fifty feet further down the sidewalk, and there lay another folded bill. I was adept at picking up bills and quickly scooped it up. It too had tens on each corner. Beyond feeling lucky, my brain quickly added the tens and told me that twenty dollars was the exact cost of a train ticket to Chicago. I watched the local paper to see if anyone was reporting the loss. I may have only found a portion of what was lost, but to get even a portion back would be helpful. However, at the end of two weeks there were no items in the lost-and-found section of the paper. Then I earmarked the money for a train ticket. Was somebody looking out for me? What if Dad's car had been operable that day?

Here in early August, Jean and I were trying to finalize our wedding plans, mostly by phone. That twenty dollars I found was just itching to be spent on a train ticket to Chicago. As my planned marriage to Jean so soon after my military discharge had caused some strain within the family, things got a little more strained today when brother Bud informed us that he and Hap, his fiancée, were going to be married on the thirtieth of that month. That was just two weeks before our wedding day. Bud and Hap (Emily) had been engaged for quite some time and were both students at Slippery Rock State Teachers College, so marrying before school started probably made sense if they had the means to pay for living quarters.

Jean informed me that two of her high school classmates had agreed to be ushers in our wedding, John Coburn and Bill McConnell. My best man would be Bob Walker, one of my high school classmates and a good friend. Bob and I had been chemistry partners and teammates in basketball. We had gone to the war program auto-mechanic school the last three months of our senior year. Jean's twin sister, Jane, would be maid of honor, with sister Laura and my sister, Audrey, being bridesmaids.

I chose a weekend and went off to Glen Ellyn to be with Jean. She had the weekend off and our station was closed on Sundays, so it was a most convenient time. This would be our last get-together before our wedding week, so we spent it on some final preparations. Back home, there was Bud and Hap's wedding coming up, and for me, I had not yet found a place for Jean and me to live. She was anxious about that. Time ran out quickly, and I returned home for the other wedding.

Bud and Hap were married in her home in Ebensburg, Pennsylvania. The Redman family were great hosts, and the wedding went off without a hitch. The newlyweds had to squeeze in a honeymoon and then make it to Illinois for our wedding.

Finally our day was close at hand, two days away. Bob Walker and Audrey would be coming in by train. Mom, Dad, and the newlyweds would be driving in. I had been here in Glen Ellyn for several days. With no automobile, I did not know what to plan for a honeymoon. Jean's mom and dad generously allowed us to take their family car on our honeymoon. They would be staying home. This was a real sacrifice for them, because there were three workers who depended on Mom to take them to the train and then pick them up after work. Since we would have a car, we chose Wisconsin Dells as the place to spend our honeymoon. I had never heard of the Dells, but from what people were telling me, it was "a place to go" for honeymooners in the Midwest, much like Easterners went to Niagara Falls. It sounded good to me, and was only possible because of a generous family.

Our Wedding

This was the day, September 14, 1946, our wedding day. Bob Walker and Audrey arrived early that morning. I stayed with the Ludwigs overnight so that I would not get to see the bride before the wedding. The Ludwigs were longtime friends of the family and were about two blocks away from Jean's home. Bob got to meet Jean before coming to see me, while Audrey stayed at the Simpsons. Time was dragging and anxiety was getting higher. We got word that Mom, Dad, and the newlyweds had arrived safely in Glen Ellyn, relieving me of some anxiety. The wedding was scheduled for three o'clock that afternoon at Saint Mark's Episcopal Church, a mile away. The wedding reception would be in fellowship hall, there in the church. Father Williams, Jean's pastor, was out of town, so Father Gibson would stand in for him. He was a lifelong friend of Mom Simpson, and had been her pastor as a child.

As the clock neared three, along with Bob, my best man, and ushers John and Bill, we walked into the sanctuary, which was filled to capacity, with some standees along the outer walls. At the appointed hour, the organist began the music, during which the bridesmaids would be coming down the center aisle. Father Gibson moved to his place at the center, but nothing happened. No bridesmaids appeared. Five minutes, still no action. Ten minutes, no action. Father Gibson, at age eighty-two, told me he was going to sit down. At fifteen minutes, no one had come down that aisle, and anxiety was near its peak as I thought about the railroad crossing between home and church. Could there have been an accident? During this waiting period, the bridesmaids became visible at the entrance to the sanctuary, but there was no music, only silence, My knees were wobbling; I was near panic. At twenty minutes past three, Jean's mother walked down the aisle and sat down.

The music began again as Audrey, Laura, and Jane, in timely fashion, came forward down the aisle. Then the sanctuary was filled with the sound of the wedding march as Jean appeared at the entrance on her father's arm and moved down the aisle toward the chancel area, as Father Gibson arose and took his place. I was in awe of her beauty as she approached, and in what was about to happen between the two of us, a moment never to be forgotten. Praise God!

Father Gibson, after charging us, asked, "Charles Frederick, wilt thou have this woman to be thy wedded wife, to live together after God's ordinance in the holy estate of matrimony?" along with other appropriate inquiry, which he also directed to Ruth Jean, using "wedded husband" in order. After receiving Jean's hand from Dad Simpson, Father Gibson proceeded to marry us as we exchanged vows and performed the giving and receiving rings.

He said, "Those whom God hath joined together let no man put asunder," then pronounced us as man and wife. How truly God has blessed us through a remarkable set of circumstances.

Following the wedding, we rejoiced in the celebration shared by all at our wedding reception, which included Ed, the train conductor whom I had met in the early days of our courtship. Ed took many wonderful pictures of our wedding party. What a truly nice gentleman. In the midst of the celebration, Mom, Dad, Audrey, and the newlyweds (Bud and Hap) had to head back to Pennsylvania. The wedding party made a quick trip to the photo studio for formal poses. With the reception over, we went back to the house and changed into more casual dress for the home reception, dominated mostly by older friends of Jean's parents, who were really nice people.

As to why the bride had been twenty minutes late for our wedding, everyone had left the house thinking Jean and Mom were in one of the other's car. Wrong! With some delay at the church, they realized what had happened. A driver had to be called from his seat in church for a hurried trip back to the house.

All is well that ends well, but for the rest of our lives we would always be married twenty minutes less than we had planned.

The evening was drawing to a close, so Jean and I went to get our luggage and leave for our honeymoon. All our luggage was missing. Of course, this was a prank, but it did not sit well with the newlyweds. There was no use of us looking for it; it could be anywhere. After a tiring, though joyous day, we decided to just sit still while everyone had their laughs. Then someone went across the street to Bill McConnell's (one of the ushers) house and retrieved the luggage from his porch. We put the luggage in the family sedan and drove away. We had reservations at a hotel in Saint Charles, Illinois, which was not too far away. It was not far enough away to rule out further pranks at the hotel, but nothing happened. We checked in and spent the first night of our lives together, in a different fashion than on those night trains between Chicago and Pittsburgh. All in all, we felt that we had a most wonderful wedding, capped off with many gifts and good wishes, which included a wedding gift from Art's family, the Uhlemans. That was very special.

As dawn's early light filtered in the window, we were ready for "our first day." It was Sunday morning and there was no restaurant in the hotel, so we drove away to find a place for breakfast. I had no familiarity with towns or places in most of Illinois or Wisconsin, so it was great to have been supplied with the vital road maps needed for our planned trip to the Wisconsin Dells. We did not have reservations, but had no trouble finding a room at the hotel. After last night's stay in Saint Charles, I told Jean that the town was named after me, my formal name being Charles. She was not impressed or believing. I guess I should try to be more "saintly."

Our honeymoon was going so well, and we were so in love. We spent much of the day on a tour boat along the river, which afforded us spectacular views of the rock formations not visible from any other venue. We took in a water show and spent time seeing other sights in the vicinity. After several days at the Dells and a night in Madison, we came back to Glen Ellyn, finding cowbells attached to our bedsprings.

Red Remaley—Boston, MA, 1944

Red Remaley—Post-war picture, Verona, PA, June 1946

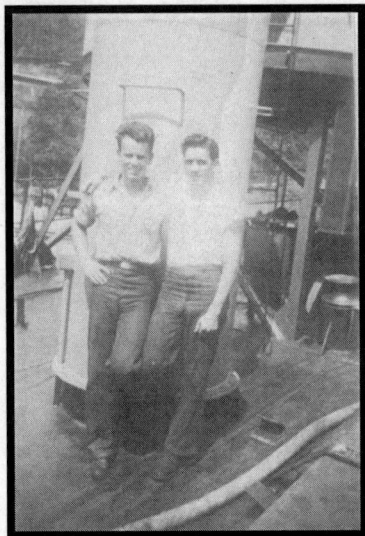

Red with Art Quimiro on Art's ship, USS *LST-631*,
in Hollandia, New Guinea, June 30, 1945

Red Remaley—New Caledonia, 1945

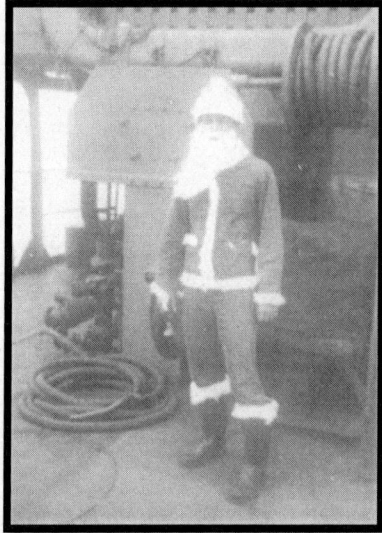

Red as Santa on USS *LST-1024*—Christmas 1945

Clyde L. (Bud) Remaley, Naval air cadet—1944

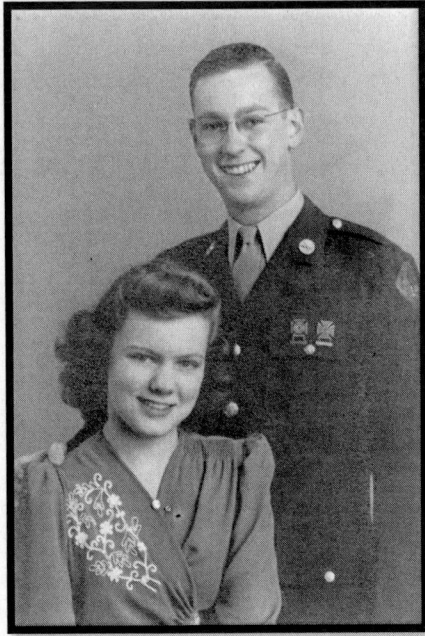

Jean Simpson and Arthur Uhleman—1944

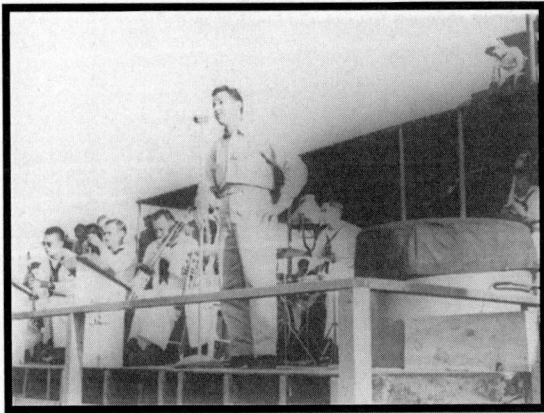

**Aboard USS *LST-1024* in June 1945,
New Caledonia, the Dennis Day show. Note:
John Fritz is on the extreme right with the bass fiddle.**

The first photo Red received from Jean Simpson, age nineteen, during their year-and-a-half correspondence

Jean Simpson in her
Red Cross uniform—Glen Ellyn, IL, 1944

Jean Simpson and Red Remaley—Glen Ellyn, IL, 1946

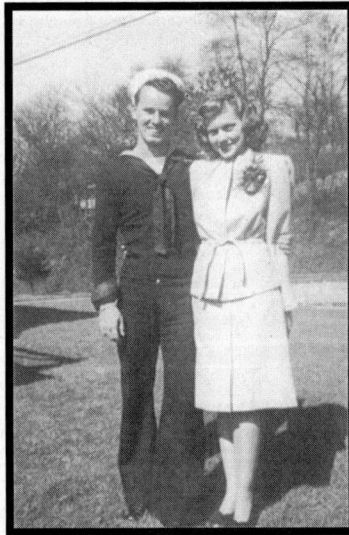

Red and Jean in Verona, PA, during Easter 1946.
This was Red's first visit back to his
hometown since he entered the Navy in 1943.

Wedding day in Glen Ellyn, IL—September 14, 1946
Left to right: Jane Simpson (Jean's twin sister),
Jean Simpson Remaley, Laura Simpson

Red and Jean Remaley—September 14, 1946, in Glen Ellyn, IL

Bridal party—September 14, 1946, in Glen Ellyn, IL
Left to right: Carol Rowland (flower girl), Jean
Simpson Remaley, Jane Simpson (standing), Laura
Simpson, Audrey Remaley

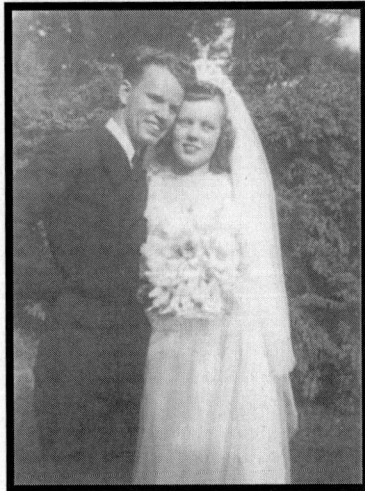

Newlyweds—September 14, 1946,
in Glen Ellyn, IL. Jean is wearing the necklace
with the cross, given to her by Art Uhleman.

Red and Jean Remaley purchased this
first home in August 1947, in Verona, PA.

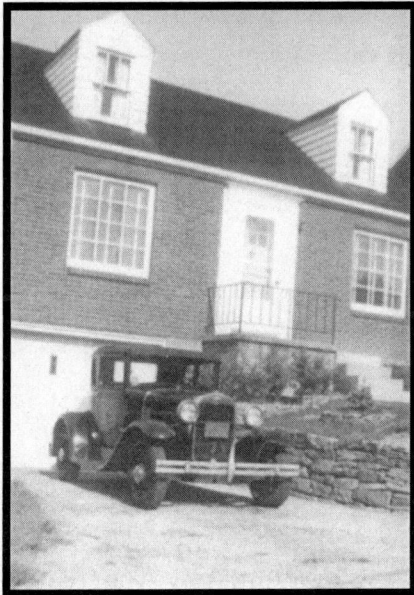

In 1948, Red and Jean bought their
first car together, a 1930 Ford Model A.

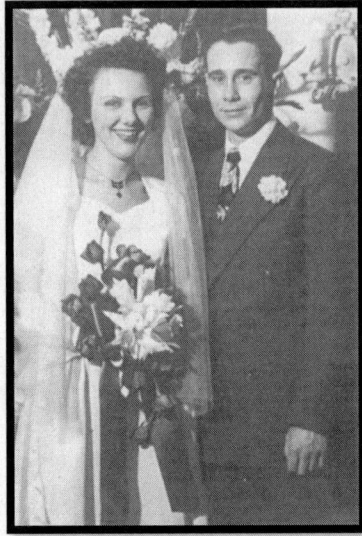

Laura Simpson Ritter and Frank Ritter on their
wedding day in February 1948, in Glen Ellyn, IL

Jean, Carol, and Red Remaley in their living room in 1952

Christmas 1954, in Glen Ellyn, IL—
Red, Carol, Jean, and Robert Remaley

Jean's parents, Ruth (age sixty-four) and
Warren (age seventy-one) Simpson—February 6, 1965

Red and Jean moved into their second
home in 1955 and have remained there ever since.

Graduation days—In June 1965, Red Remaley
completed his studies and was ordained a Methodist
minister at age thirty-nine. At the same time, his
daughter, Carol, graduated from high school.

Lynn and Carol Johnson's wedding day on
December 26, 1969, at the Green Valley United
Methodist Church, North Versailles, PA
Left to right: Reverend Charles "Red" Remaley Jr.,
Jean Remaley, Carol Remaley Johnson, Lynn
Johnson, Carol and Robert Johnson (Lynn's parents)

The garage built by Red in 1972

Our motor home—Red, Jean, and Jack Felger, Red's former shipmate and lifelong friend (October 1982)

Elizabeth (Betty) and
Charles (Chuck) F. Remaley Sr., Red's parents

Fiftieth wedding anniversary
in 1996—Red and Jean Remaley

Carol and Lynn Johnson on a cruise in 1999

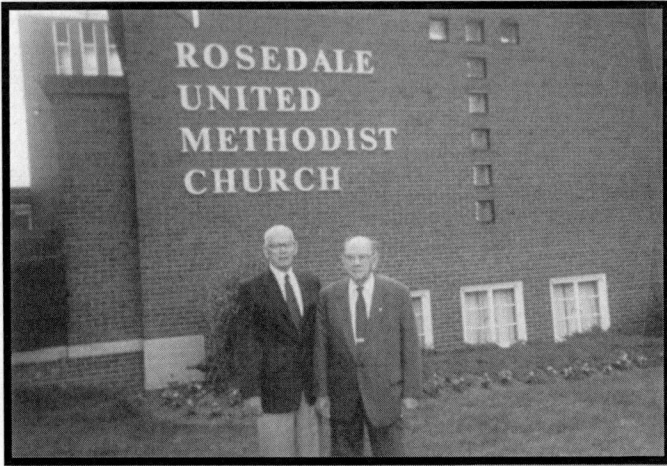

This June 2000 photo shows Red and his father,
Chuck Remaley, in front of the Rosedale United
Methodist Church, Penn Hills, PA. In 1960, Red began
his ministerial career here as the assistant minister.

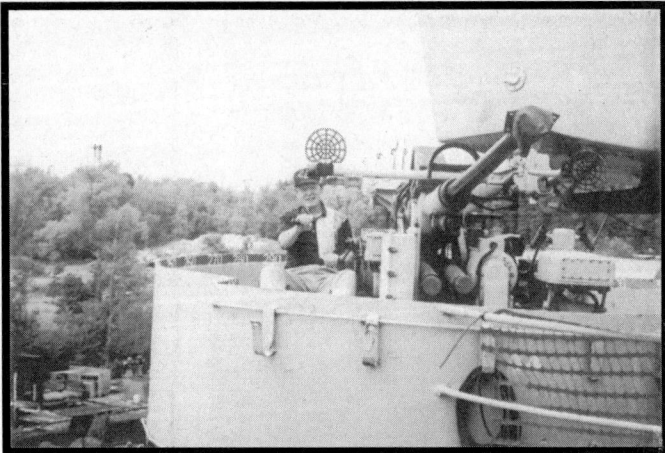

Red aboard USS *LST-325* docked in
Mobile, AL, in 2002, showing the gunner's
position he held aboard USS *LST-1024* in World War II

The Remaley siblings—December 21, 2003
Left to right: Bud Remaley (age eighty), Audrey Remaley
Davis (age seventy-six), Red Remaley (age seventy-eight)

Jane Simpson Beers and
Jim Beers—2005, Lake Arrowhead, GA

Jack and Mamie Felger—2005, Verona, PA

Bob and Debbie Remaley—Christmas 2007

The Remaleys: Bob, Red, Carol, Jean—Christmas 2007

Carol and Lynn Johnson—Christmas 2007

Jean Remaley (age eighty-four)—
2010 Navy Reunion in Pittsburgh, PA

Red and Jean Remaley (both age eighty-nine)—2014

About Our Future

The honeymoon was over, in that we went away together and came back to "square one." The honeymoon was a beginning, not an end. "Together forever" is what we felt in our hearts. Each day in this marriage was a step toward that "forever," which would be what God deemed it to be. We would be ill prepared for all those tomorrows if we did not pause in the present to acknowledge the improbability of us ever meeting, let alone being united in holy matrimony. This was not a script written by man, but of God. That Spirit that brought us together must be within us in order to sustain us.

Through the pages of this book, the parts of the whole have been documented little by little from the time a young soldier and the author became friends in a faraway war. People and circumstances came into play in a way that one would almost believe it to be "made up." A romance such as ours is probably dotted by a few "what-ifs" and "but fors." However, love came to the fore in its inimitable way, and by God's grace we would play out our role in His scheme of things. Here, in Glen Ellyn, we looked back on our wonderful honeymoon aided by the use of the Simpsons' family car. Life has a way of removing roadblocks and mysteriously solving our problems. Not expecting to have a car on our honeymoon was one of those roadblocks.

Jean and I knew we had a major task ahead of us to get all our shower and wedding gifts, along with her personal belongings and clothes, to Pennsylvania. However, we just got a phone call from John Clawson, the man who supplied our station with recapped tires. He was calling from La Grange, Illinois, a town not far from Glen Ellyn. Knowing that John was coming to this area, my dad suggested he call here to see if we would like him to haul our things to Pennsylvania. He was driving a pickup truck. Can you believe this? This good fortune was beyond anything we could have imagined. I gave John a resounding yes, and he said he would be here tomorrow morning.

This place was a madhouse as we gathered together everything we had planned on taking to our new home, which at the moment would be in residence with my parents. I had given serious thought, and with deep gratitude, this momentous happening in Jean's life, that through her love for me, she was saying yes to this journey in an unfamiliar place that lay ahead of her. It was an awesome responsibility for me to assure that our life together would be worth every sacrifice she was making. I was so overwhelmed by her love and beauty, especially her inner beauty, which shone through all she did and said. I believed she was incapable of creating a divisive situation. She would be loved by my family and friends.

As we loaded everything into John's truck, I was so amazed at all the blessings in life that come at the "right time." The odds had been against John's timely visit to La Grange just when we needed his help, but still it had happened. My Silent Partner kept pulling the strings. We thanked John as he pulled away, heading for Pennsylvania. With most of our belongings in his truck, we gathered the "leftovers" for our trip tomorrow morning, as Mom had volunteered to drive us to Pennsylvania. Things were going smooth, with so many wonderful blessings paving the way.

After a long and exhausting trip, we arrived safely in Verona, thanks to Mom Simpson. Of course, John got there a day ahead of us, so we had a lot of sorting to do. We had a spacious bedroom, which would be our "apartment" until we found a permanent place to live. We had no furniture, so as soon as living quarters turned up we would have major shopping to do. I know we were burdening my parents at the moment, but I just prayed that all would work out okay. With my mother doing all the cooking, I was sure she was hopeful we would be on a short stay. Jean was anxious to get our own place. She joked about her lack of experience in the kitchen— she was getting acquainted with her mother-in-law.

I had settled in to the daily routine of working at the service station. It was not a booming business, but we were helped immeasurably by having a local steel company as one of our customers. There were also some small businesses who ran accounts with us. While at the station, I constantly thought about how Mom and Jean were doing, and how desperately we needed to find an apartment. Nearly a week had passed with no leads.

Surely my Silent Partner was looking out for us. Today I got a phone call from Mary Dasta, sister of my friend Al Torchia, who had been a German prisoner of war. She informed me that the second and third floor in an old house next door to her were available for rent. We quickly inquired about it and were accepted as tenants at sixty-four dollars a month including utilities. Since we had no debts, we were sure we could do very well. Buses ran both directions past the apartment, which was great because we did not have a car.

We began shopping for furniture. Our first stop was at the E. N. Miller Furniture Company here in Verona, my employer at the time of my induction into the Navy in 1943. There was a strong demand for new furniture because of the high number of young couples being married following the war. Most industries had to revert to what they had produced in peacetime. Likewise, our mothers left war-production jobs and returned to being full-time homemakers, Mom Simpson from working in a radio factory and my mom from a job in a steel mill. The return to normalcy was taking a long time, but businesses were cashing in on their backlog of orders. We needed a bedroom suite, a living room suite, a kitchen set, and a stove. We also needed a refrigerator, but none were available; you had to join a waiting list. Miller's had one bedroom suite that appealed to us, so Alex Wiley, our salesman and my friend, put a "Sold" sign on it. In a good selection of kitchen sets, we found one with much chrome trimmed in red, so it received a sold ticket. He then sold us a nice gas stove.

Alex apologized for the lack of selection in living room furnishings; indeed, he pointed out the poor quality of what he had available. He sold us a beautiful nine-by-twelve-foot burgundy rug for our living room and suggested we go to Kauffman's department store in Pittsburgh for a living room suite. We took his advice and found a nice matching sofa and chair done in blue mohair. We added to it a rose-colored occasional chair. Our lack of a refrigerator had been filled by the gift of an old-fashioned icebox and an iceman to deliver ice.

I must digress while I have these dealings with the E. N. Miller Company. For many years, I thought I was an adopted child. First, I did not resemble my parents or my siblings. I was the second son in our family, but I was named after my father, which added "Junior" to my name. Why was my brother not named after my father? I was never called Charles, my given name, but "Brother," which I came to believe was used to make me feel more of a part of the family. This odd name was used until I was in third grade at school when the "number-one son" became embarrassed about calling me "Brother" in public, so he began calling me "Red," as I had red hair. I had a happy childhood in a very good family, but over the years I noticed things strengthening my belief that I was adopted. I never discussed these feelings with anyone.

At the age of seventeen, I had a job delivering furniture for the E. N. Miller Company. I was part of a two-man crew on the truck. One day, we were delivering a room of furniture to the Croyle family in New Kensington, who were total strangers to me. This delivery required many trips between truck and house, and each time I entered the house I sensed that Mrs. Croyle and her daughter were having a discussion, which ended with a snicker as I entered the room. I was curious, so I asked if we were causing a problem. The mother said she was discussing my identity with her daughter, and the more she saw of me, the more she was convinced I was a Remaley. When I admitted she was correct in her assumption, she told me a story that lifted a burden from my mind. As a child, her best friend had been a girl named Sadie Remaley, and in me she saw such a resemblance to Sadie that she bet her daughter I was a Remaley. Sadie was my dad's sister. This encounter assured me that I was indeed a Remaley, and a veil of doubt was lifted. What a small world, what a wonderful world!

Day by day, our furniture was delivered to our apartment. We added all our wedding and shower gifts to the making of an apartment into a home. We did not have a private entrance; we had access by using the landlord's front door. As telephones were hard to come by, we would be without basic communication. There was no privacy door into our second floor at the top of the stairs, which was rather scary, as anyone visiting the landlord could easily barge in on us. Of course, it also gave easy access to the landlord in our absence. When apartments were so hard to find, you had to learn to live with some inconveniences. We were grateful to have this place to live.

On the second floor, there was a living room, quite large with an adjoining alcove about seven by ten feet, which could allow for a folding bed for guests. There was a large bathroom and a fair-size kitchen on this floor. A large bedroom filled the third-floor area, which was great because our bedroom suite took up all the available space. We stocked our shelves with the basic food items to get us started.

Tonight we loaded Dad's car with all our clothes and moved in. We lacked closet space, but would be getting a large, portable, hardboard closet. Now we were at home. We were so happy, and so in love. Already, I was concerned that Jean would not be too lonely as I went out to work in the morning. Not having a phone was terribly unhandy for me to call and check on her. The station is a mile away, and Mom and Dad lived three blocks away. Using Dad's car, I would be able to come home for lunch, which would be great in helping Jean be comfortable in our life together. It was such a radical change in her life, indeed, a leap of faith. She amazed me the way she adapted in these earliest days here in Pennsylvania.

The weeks were rolling by and the weather was turning cold. Once in a while, weather permitting, Jean and I would walk over to Oakmont to see a movie. The theatre was about a mile and a half away. We returned home on the bus. Our grocery store was about three quarters of a mile away, a nice walk if the bags were not too heavy. There were times when our friend Frank Ritter got his dad's car on a Sunday afternoon and we would go for a ride, with Jim Beers accompanying us. These two men had been my friends since childhood. Neither of them was married, nor did they have girlfriends.

Jean's mom and dad were here for Thanksgiving, and they came equipped with a cot and rollaway bed to sleep on in that alcove off the living room. This was a most welcome visit, as Jean came from such a close-knit family, and they were not used to separation. Thanksgiving dinner went well, with mother and daughter sharing in the preparation. Mom and Dad's visit was short but important, first for Jean and then for them to see our home and furnishings.

There was a group of young women, most of whom had been a year ahead of me in high school, who met monthly just to keep their friendship alive. They had invited Jean to join them. I cannot begin to describe what a blessing this was to Jean and to me. For Jean, it was like a window on the local world and what was going on in the community.

We had no debt, but neither did we have much of a balance in our checking account. This had come to be as we spent most all my savings purchasing furniture. I am thankful we had that nest egg to allow us to get all the necessities to furnish our apartment. My weekly income of thirty-five dollars was sufficient to meet current expenses, but did not leave any room for saving for the future. I wondered what we would do in an emergency, say a costly illness. Today, that concern was somewhat lifted when my Uncle Bob, Dad's brother, stopped at the station. He called me aside and said that he thought Jean and I could, in our young age and being newly married, easily face a financial crisis. He wanted us to know that he and Aunt Twila were here to help us should the need occur. Wow! Can you imagine that? To have such special people willing to help us was an immeasurable blessing, and so timely.

When I came home from work, Jean was upset. I had forgotten to empty the pan under the icebox and it had overflowed, leaking down to the first floor and soaking the newly wallpapered ceiling in the landlord's dining room. The landlord, Mrs. Pavone, came upstairs and blamed Jean for the problem. I apologized to her and assured her it would not happen again. However, I did not offer to repair any damage, which caused tension between us. I felt sorry for Jean as she bore the brunt of my forgetting to empty that pan. This would not be the last of our problems. I tried to comfort Jean as I told her about Uncle Bob's visit at the station, and she was quite pleased over their "backing" us. Uncle Bob was a veteran of World War I, and probably a veteran of an early marriage.

With Christmas behind us, Jean and I were moving ahead with our plans for a New Year's weekend in Glen Ellyn. We, of course, would be going by train. Jean cleared it with Mom to allow us to bring Jim Beers and Frank Ritter with us. Arriving in Chicago, we were met by sisters Laura and Jane. Early in the day, Jim teamed with Laura and Frank with Jane, but as the hours passed they switched, Frank with Laura, Jim with Jane. Was something serious going on? The high point of the weekend was a party on the eve of the new year, arranged by Laura and Jane with many friends of the Simpson sisters. It was a great holiday for all of us, especially for Jean, as she was back home for the first time since our marriage and honeymoon. On the Pennsylvania-bound train, we learned that Jim and Frank planned to keep in touch with Laura and Jane.

Back at my job at the station, it started out as a normal day until Norm Sellers came in for gas. As I was cleaning his windshield, he engaged me in conversation about my future in the business of pumping gas. Maybe I had not concerned myself enough with the future; I was so wrapped up in love to realize I needed this talk with Norm. He was a longtime employee of the Bell Telephone Company of Pennsylvania and proceeded to inform me that his company was now hiring a lot of veterans. That conversation changed my life. He told me where to put in an application for employment. I thanked him for the information as he pulled away. I talked to Jean and Dad about this opportunity, and both agreed I should pursue it. In reality, the station had enough business to support one family, but not quite enough to support two without increasing the number of operating hours. Another one of those timely incidents in my life. My Silent Partner sure was kept busy looking out for me.

I applied for employment right away and soon received a call from Paul Loub at the employment office asking me to come in with my discharge papers and birth certificate. I was hired to start work on February 3, 1947, at a weekly wage of twenty-eight dollars, a seven-dollar cut in weekly pay. However, there was help called "on-the-job training," which was a veteran's program that, when approved, would add to my income. Also, every three months I would get a weekly three-dollar raise and one week of vacation after six months on the job. My job title in starting would be cable splicer's helper. I reported for work at the Spahr Street garage in the city of Pittsburgh and was put on a truck with George Shumm and Harry Magill, George a splicer and Harry a helper. Theirs was a troubleshooting job, which took them out over a wide area. The weather was bitter cold, and I was rather short on foul-weather gear. Having spent the past couple of years in warmer climates, this felt like the coldest February on record. One last thing Norm Sellers had told me: "I hope they do not start you out as a splicer's helper." Starting at the bottom, there wasn't anywhere to go but up.

Speaking of cold weather, Jean said it was cold enough in the staircase going to the third floor that Jell-O would set if the door were kept closed. There was no heater in our bedroom. Jean was right, as in her experiment the Jell-O set firmly.

Occasionally, when I was at the service station full time and still worked there on Saturdays, Jean would walk down to see me. Not long after one of her visits, she was engaged in conversation

114

with the landlord, who complimented her on our beautiful burgundy rug. Who knew how often our apartment was visited while we were away. It would be nice on the day we had our own home and the privacy that went with it. In those years following World War II, there was an agency that tracked the amount of rent people were paying in relation to the accommodations supplied. They checked up on our landlord and informed her she was overcharging us. What an explosion! She thought we had filed a grievance against them, when in fact, we did not even know there was such an agency. Trying to convince Mrs. Pavone and her son, whom I have known most of my life, that we were not guilty seemed to fall on deaf ears. It was my habit each morning as I left for work to come off the porch and walk straight down the lawn to the bus stop. The morning after that explosive encounter, as I walked down the lawn, I could hear Mrs. Pavone shouting at me and coming up behind me waving her broom at me. She told me to get off her lawn. This helped to build on the tension that began with that overflow of the icebox pan. To keep the peace, I stayed clear of her lawn.

In April, we found out Jean was pregnant and expecting in mid-November 1947. This was a good-news/bad-news situation. Having a child was good news, but raising our child in this apartment was bad news. This situation weighed heavy on us, and we were both short on a solution. The three-dollar raise coming at the end of April was not going to help much. We pondered over what to do over a period of several weeks when Jean came home from her ladies' night out with those who had invited her to be a part of their monthly get-together. That night's meeting was held at Betty Ann Richey's home on Shannon Road, just a few blocks away. In attendance that evening was Barbara Jo Arnold, whose father-in-law was a building contractor. The contractor's name was Lewis Arnold, a friend of my parents. It was revealed by Barbara that Mr. Arnold was ready to break ground for two new homes just a few doors away from the Richeys'. This was exciting news for me, as I viewed it in the light of Jean's pregnancy and the less-than-

helper, but with little notice I would be told to report to work at a particular location somewhere in the eastern section of Pittsburgh. Without a car and with little knowledge of the city streets, I had difficulty finding my way to the assigned work location. I would leave our apartment and catch a bus into the city, then one or two trolleys to the work site. Then I would reverse the procedure to get back home. My job was to assist the splicer in every way possible and learn the techniques of his job with the hope of advancing to his job level. In the course of any given day, the job site could be changed as he completed the work he began in the morning. Then I had to figure out which trolley to take back to where I could catch a homeward-bound bus. Oh, how I wished we had a car.

There were different news items cropping up. Jim Beers had decided that he wanted to be a dental technician. He enrolled in a school in Chicago to study for this vocation. And, get this, he was going to live with Jean's parents. That would put him pretty close to sister Jane, to say the least. That was good news for these lovers. I hoped they would not have any disagreements. Another news item was the state of Pennsylvania was getting set to pay a bonus to those who served in World War II. Frank and Laura were getting serious; I would not be surprised if they announced wedding plans in the near future. Frank was a plumber and worked in his dad's business, so he was well set in a good trade.

Jean had been having regular checkups with Dr. Aronson for her pregnancy. All was going well with her, and I thought she looked more beautiful every day. I loved her so. What a blessing that we would be in our own home before our baby came. We were both anxious about moving.

Homeowners

Almost every evening Jean and I walked over to the building site. Up till now we could walk through the house and be up to date on the progress. This evening we were locked out. Today the new permanent doors had been installed with locks, so we had to assume the interior was nearing completion. The plastering had been done for several days, and it was possible they had begun to lay the oak flooring and did not want us "snoopers" messing things up.

With about five weeks to go till move-in time, I had to approach Uncle Bob and Aunt Twila about borrowing four hundred dollars toward the closing costs. It would be a debt that would hang over our heads for a while, but it was the only answer to the problem facing us. Speaking of problems, we created another one with Mrs. Pavone. Jean and I had gone out for the day with Jim and Frank. When we got back to the apartment, a stepladder was lying across the steps leading to the front door. Early in the day, someone had painted the front porch. We were not informed of this roadblock ahead of time, and were "painted out" of our apartment. I touched the paint and found it to be only slightly tacky, so we walked over it and into the front door. As we started up the stairs, we were greeted by a screaming landlord. She told us we should have gone to her back door instead of walking on the new paint. I told her it was exactly what we would have done had she forewarned us of the affair in the first place. I also informed her we would be moving out on August 1. Right or wrong, we just hoped this was our last unpleasant encounter.

In so many places, during my time in the Navy, someone would come in over a loudspeaker and say, "Now hear this." It would be followed by some sort of message. Now hear this! In today's mail, I received a check from the US Navy—in the amount of four hundred dollars. This money was a payment for the clothes I lost in San Francisco Bay. I forgot about that claim I had filed in March 1946. Better late than never!

This was so overwhelming. How could this timing be any better, and the amount be any more perfect (unless it would have been for $401)? We had been so blessed. I give praise to my Silent Partner. We so wanted to avoid any debt beyond a mortgage payment, and through this settlement we would escape any further burden. It was good we were not struggling with a car payment; a car was not in our future anytime soon.

Being in the clear on having the funds to settle on closing day, we were gradually getting some packing done. We had to be careful not to pack anything we would need before moving day. This was one of those times when it would be nice to have had a first-floor apartment so as not to have all these steps to negotiate while carrying a stove or some other heavy furniture. We were running out of packing boxes, but expected to pick some up at the grocery store. It was hard to believe how much we had accumulated in so few months of marriage.

Along with Mr. Arnold, Jean and I met with the mortgage company and inked a thirty-year mortgage with monthly payments of sixty-seven dollars, which included taxes, interest, and little principal. With no other debt, we could manage this along with utilities as we faced the birth of our child in mid-November. We now had the keys to our new home. Mr. Arnold said there were a couple of minor items left to do. We would be moving in two days.

Well, here we were in our brand-new home without any electricity; the power company was a day late. We were about one hundred feet away from Jean's friend Betty Ann Richey. Betty's husband, Bob, and I had run some extension cords for temporary lighting. It was good that we had a gas stove. One of those "minor" items Mr. Arnold had not defined was that the toilet seat had not been installed. I was glad it was not winter, for that toilet bowl would be a little colder on the bum. We needed a strong grip on the edge of the bathtub to keep from slipping backward—H-E-L-P!

Well, we just got the news, as expected—Frank and Laura had decided to get married in March of 1948. That was around seven months away. They would be married in Glen Ellyn and take up residence here in Verona. They would be living in a home owned by Frank's parents, so they would not have a mortgage. Further, that home was only a half mile away, an easy walking distance. How wonderful for Jean to have a sister living so close. It was overwhelming for Mom and Dad Simpson to have lost two daughters to the state of Pennsylvania.

Jim had made his move. He was now in residence with the Simpsons and would soon begin his studies to be a dental technician. They had a fine home, but it had only one bathroom. With four people having to catch the train every morning, a bathroom schedule was in order.

Our power was connected a day late, but we managed through the delay. The lack of a toilet seat, now in its fifth day, was more than inconvenient. I feared for Jean; in her condition, she might have an accident. How could such a common item be in short supply? Like our apartment, closet space was almost nonexistent, so I had converted the linen closet into space for hanging clothes. Outside there was much to do; the landscaping was skimpy at best, but in time I would improve it. It was such a blessing to have this home. In our wildest dreams, we could not have expected to have our own home before our first anniversary.

On the seventh day in our new home, I arrived from work to the smiling face of my lovely wife. She met me at the door, shouting, "You will never guess what happened today."

It was obvious she had not given birth, so I asked, "What happened?"

"We got a new toilet seat," she replied.

We rejoiced together over this news. Can you imagine such a "ta-do" over a toilet seat? Believe me, this was an important happening in the Remaley household.

Mom and Dad Simpson were coming to see us near the end of the month. They informed us that a baby's crib and mattress would be supplied by them, along with many of the basic items for a newborn. This was great news, because these initial costs, though necessary, would be a strain on our budget. We were so grateful. Jean was so happy with all that was happening: Mom and Dad's visit, a baby on the way, Laura's wedding, and her planned move to Pennsylvania. With job stability and all these happenings, I too was very happy.

I had mentioned that Mr. Arnold was building two houses. They were next door to each other. The new owners of the other house moved in today. The new neighbors were Tom and Jeanette Tumulty. What a small world—Tom and I played on the same baseball team around the age of twelve. Tom was the pitcher and I was the catcher. I had never met his wife, but had seen her on the bus several times. At least we were in the same age group. Tom worked for a roofing company. On the other side of us was a vacant lot.

Our home was situated on Shannon Road. During most of my young life, we had called it the "old coal road" because there was a constant flow of coal trucks travelling in each direction. There was a now great number of concrete trucks supplanting the dominance of the coal trucks, due to the boom in new-home construction. It was quite dangerous to walk this road, for there were no sidewalks and the road was narrow. My parents lived about four blocks away on the same road. It was a rather steep hill to walk in paying them a visit.

With no car, and Jean's pregnancy, we did not go to the movies at this time, but we enjoyed our evenings together listening to the radio. At least we had a telephone to keep in touch with friends and relatives. Being without a telephone in the apartment had been restrictive in that Jean could not call her family without using my parents' phone. For the same reason, Mom and Dad Simpson could not call Jean. A four-party line had its issues, but for the present we were just happy to have this means of communication.

Nearly a full month had passed since we moved in, and we were now entertaining our first guests, Jean's parents. They were more than pleased with our new home. We had set up the cot and rollaway bed in our future dining room to accommodate them. This would also be the baby's room when that time came. Mom was planning to take Jean shopping to buy all those incidental items for our baby that only an experienced mother would remember as necessary, especially a mother of twins. Mom was so good hearted; I was sure she would buy some outfits for Jean. My precious wife was doing a great job of getting the most out of all the clothes she had brought from Illinois. I prayed for an increase in our buying power, but we had to be patient.

Mom and Jean came home loaded after their shopping trip. She bought two really nice maternity dresses, which were sorely needed. I did not believe we would want for anything concerning our baby's needs, after viewing what had been purchased today. Things had gone so right for Jean and me since the day we professed our love for each other. At every turn, some person or something came on stage to fill a need. It was so overwhelming to be so blessed.

Frank showed a lot of attention toward Mom and Dad, as did his parents by taking them out or inviting them to dinner. My parents, on the other hand, seemed somewhat distant to Jean's parents. I did not know why. In reality, my dad was the only family member who seemed to genuinely care that Jean was a member of our family. I prayed that improvement was near at hand; I felt uncomfortable over this. Jean did not comment about this situation, but was always patient and kind to all.

We enjoyed Mom and Dad's visit. It was certainly too short for Jean, but I believed they would come back soon after their grandchild was born. So much had happened in the past year that it was hard to keep track. There was our wedding, Laura and Jane falling in love with Frank and Jim, a pregnancy, a new home, and the announcement of Laura and Frank's wedding plans. Our first anniversary was just a few days away. How time flies.

Coming home from work today, I thought about this special day, September 14, 1947, our first anniversary. Jean greeted me with a hug and a kiss. She looked so beautiful, even in a maternity dress, and she was so special. We were not able to go out to celebrate, but would have a meaningful evening together. I looked upon Jean as the greatest gift any man could have. I reflected upon the many things that had brought us to this day: my friendship with Art, his death in battle, a letter to his family, letters from his mother and Jean. As Jean and I had corresponded over the months, we had begun to have meaningful feelings toward each other, not knowing what the future had in store for us. Even my battle injury at Leyte had played a part in this drama, as it had landed me at Great Lakes Naval Hospital where we met for the first time. I shall never forget how much Mom did to help me have time with Jean during my hospital stay. I was so in love with Jean long before that first meeting, and in this short time it had grown immensely. I have heard it said many times that you cannot live on love alone, and this I agree with, but love is the engine that powered our marriage. It was not just our love for each other, but our faith and love of God.

Mom had informed Jean that Jim and Jane were talking about getting married in October of 1948. Wow! Two weddings in the same year. This script for the marrying of three Simpson sisters was unreal, but so beautiful. I prayed their marriages would be as rock solid as ours. I had to believe Jim would have second thoughts about continuing his studies to be a dental technician and look for immediate employment.

As we flipped the calendar to October, it was time to acknowledge that Jean would turn twenty-two on this first day of the month. Of course, she would be talking to twin sister Jane as they celebrated the occasion. I would not be twenty-two until the nineteenth, so for these few days I would tease her about robbing the cradle in marrying me.

The months had rolled by quite rapidly, as so many things had been happening. We were now on the threshold of parenthood as the delivery day approached, mid-November, about two weeks away. Were we ready? We would have to be, inexperienced as we were. We were as ready as any couple could be, and as I mentioned some months ago, it would be great that our child would come into this home as opposed to the apartment. Jean looked like she could deliver any day, but we would go along with Dr. Aronson's prediction. Mom Simpson had made sure that we had everything we would need on hand. I was sure Jean would be blessed with a mother's instinct—at the moment, I did not sense having a father's instinct.

What a great day! Jean gave birth to a beautiful baby girl in the Montefiore Hospital in Pittsburgh. We named her Carol Ann. She was abundantly healthy, for which we were deeply grateful. Jean was doing well and should come home with Carol in five to seven days. Today was November 13, 1947; the doctor had predicted well. How blessed we were to have Carol so early in life, so as to grow with her and still be fairly young when she reached adulthood. She was the first grandchild in the family. We were now a family of three. That had a special ring to it.

Someone once said, "Babies are for younger people." I now fully understood what they meant, as we washed baby bottles, made formula, changed diapers, burped the baby, and washed diapers, along with nighttime feeding. We were up to it, but the responsibility fell on Jean completely as I went off to work. However, we were happy and blessed. My dad was overwhelmed at being a grandpa and stopped every chance he got. Day by day, Carol grew and was strong and healthy. I believed she would be a blonde like her mother.

We had gone through Thanksgiving as if it were just another day, as we had been so busy at parenting. Both of us were pretty well organized, and Carol slept without too many night calls. As Christmas loomed ahead, I would have to check out the meager decorations we had at the apartment. Finances were tight for us, so we would not be overspending on anybody. It was hard to overcome the shortfall caused by Christmas spending. The years ahead should find us in a stronger financial position for the holiday.

We were invited to have Christmas dinner with my parents, so we were not concerned about travel plans. We spent ever so lightly on family gifts, and even lighter on ourselves. Our Christmas fund had less than ten dollars in it after buying gifts for others. We had not gotten anything for each other, and with so little cash, we pondered what to do. Our choice was simply to buy a set of steak knives at the local G. C. Murphy 5 & 10 for less than ten dollars. This was somewhat embarrassing, but we had no Christmas debt. We were happy with each other in the way we managed our affairs. All doctor and hospital bills for Carol's birth had been paid. Dinner was delicious, and it was nice to feast with family for the first time in many months. We truly counted our blessings.

This New Year's Day we were reflecting on the year just past. The high point, of course, was Carol's birth. My change in employment had brought a wonderful stability for our family with assured hospitalization and vacations, but above all, how it had been the ticket to secure a mortgage on our home. We looked back on where we had been last New Year's weekend and the joy of those romantic relationships that had developed between Laura and Frank and Jane and Jim. It had been a memorable year, filled with so many blessings, along with a joyful first anniversary.

I received a call from my shipmate and friend Jack Felger. He asked me to be his best man in his wedding on July 3, 1948. I agreed to do it. Of course, he was marrying Mamie, the young lady of willow-tree fame. They would be married in Petersburg, Ohio. Not having a car presented a real problem, but somehow I would get to the church on time. I lived closer to Jack than any of my other shipmates, so I trusted we would stick together in the years ahead.

My future brother-in-law, Jim Beers, had given up on being a dental technician. Mr. Alfred, a next-door neighbor to the Simpsons, had talked to Jim about going to work at his company, the Illinois Bell Telephone Company. What a coincidence he and I would both become telephone employees. Mr. Alfred was in management and assured Jim of a job. I hoped it worked out well for him in light of his impending marriage to Jane. My first anniversary with the phone company was yesterday, February 3. How grateful I was to Norm Sellers for tipping me off to the hiring at Bell of Pennsylvania. I was now making one dollar per hour. Things were looking up.

Laura and Frank were married early this month in Glen Ellyn and settled down here in Verona. Jean was so happy to have Laura here within walking distance. Mom and Dad were glad Laura and Jean lived in the same town, as they had to travel over five hundred miles to get here. In time, we would have many get-togethers. It would be easier if we had a car.

Some men showed up on that vacant lot next to our home today and began to stake out what looked like the beginning of a new house. We would welcome a neighbor on that site, as it was rather unsightly at present. I learned the name of the younger man, George Sprague. He and his dad were working as a team. This would be the first house they built. I hoped they would do a good job.

We got word that Jim had started on his job at the phone company. He would be working as an installer, which would involve a lot of pole climbing and in-basement work. At this point, I wished I had started as an installer, as there were no hurdles to jump in moving toward top pay. I had to qualify for splicer in order to move up from a splicer's helper.

Heavy equipment showed up next door today and made quite a large hole in the ground for the foundation of a house. With the summer weather not far away, construction was expected to move rapidly. Looking ahead, George Sprague, the contractor, asked if we would supply their water and electricity needs during construction, with appropriate reimbursement. We agreed to help them.

Our telephone service had been upgraded from a four-party line to a private line. No more of those party-line rings in the middle of the night, nor conversations on the line instead of dial tone. Happy day!

"April showers bring May flowers." That is an old saying, but it sure was true today with blossoming trees and forsythia brightening our surroundings. It was the kind of weather in which Jean would like to walk over to Laura's home, but with Carol at six months it was not an easy walk. Guess what! Today I was talking to one of my coworkers, Dave Logan, bemoaning how tough it was to not have a car.

Dave said, "I will sell you a car."

I told him I did not have any money and asked where he would get a car to sell me. He said he had a 1930 Model A Ford stored in a barn in Oakmont. In asking Dave how much he wanted for the car, he said, "Two hundred dollars."

"Money is still the issue," I told him.

"Pay me when you get the money," he replied.

Wow! This seemed so unbelievable. I pondered his offer for a few minutes. "Will you take four dollars a week?" I asked.

He said yes.

"But what if I need to buy a new tire and do not have four dollars to pay you?" I asked.

Dave told me to skip the payments until the tire was paid for. We agreed on these terms. He would pick me up tomorrow after work, and we would go to the barn, at which time he would give me the title to the car.

Here at the barn, Dave rolled open the doors, and there before my eyes was our first car. It was a coupe, black with red wheels. The car was covered with dust, but it was so beautiful, even if it was eighteen years old. Dave got in and turned the key; the engine started immediately. He told me to get in and drive it home. He followed me closely so as not to expose the fact that the car had no license plate. Safely in our driveway, I tooted the horn to get Jean's attention. What a smile she had as she came down to the driveway.

"It has a stick shift. I can drive that," she said. Jean seemed more excited than me as she gave it the once-over. It would be hard to put into words what this car meant to us.

First, could we ever use this car without being grateful to Dave Logan for his generosity in the most liberal payment terms we had ever heard of? Who knows when we would have gotten a car without him. Suddenly, we had mobility. I could drive to and from work, leaving later and getting home earlier. Jean could drive over to Laura's. We could go grocery shopping without walking or asking Dad's help in lending his car. Jean, Carol, and I could go to Jack and Mamie's wedding in a couple of weeks. It was a sixty-mile trip. We were so hyped up over this car that we did not care how old it looked beside a 1948 car. What a blessing!

A house was taking shape next door; it was up and under roof. I expected the brickwork to begin any day now. It would be done by contract, as the Spragues were not bricklayers. We had enjoyed watching father and son during the building of this house. They worked slowly, and at times, seemed uncertain about what to do next, but all in all, the house appeared to be well constructed.

Jean and Carol had gone over to Laura's several times. As time permitted, I tried to work in the yard while they were out. This evening as I worked in the yard, I could hear a "stuck" horn off in the distance. When Jean and Carol got home, I learned that it had been the horn on our new car. A neighbor disconnected a wire to stop the noise.

Tomorrow would be Jack and Mamie's wedding. We were spending the evening at the Shaffer's home, as Mamie's mother had the wedding party here for dinner. It had been an evening well spent, as it was giving us time to get better acquainted. We had scarcely seen these friends since Jack and I had got out of the Navy. Mamie's church was only about two blocks away on this same street. Jean, Carol, and I would be staying overnight with Jack's parents, Helen and Fred, at their home in New Springfield. They were such nice people, and we were thankful for their hospitality.

Recalling how Jean was twenty minutes late getting to the church for our wedding, it was comforting to see Mamie coming down the aisle on time. The wedding was just beautiful, as was the bride. I was thankful Jack honored me with the invitation to be his best man, hoping that we would be best friends for life. With the wedding in the history books, the newlyweds got in their car for a planned honeymoon to New England. Pranks were one thing, but what was done to their car was beyond being funny. Some person or persons had rubbed Limburger cheese into the car's heater core and radiator core. This was a nasty trick. I think they had to get some steam cleaning done. They did get away for about ten days.

Back home, we found the house next door nearing completion. George told me they had originally been building it for themselves, but had chosen to put it on the market. I watched his dad building a wall along the driveway. It really was not looking very good; it was of layered stone of poor quality. I chided him about its appearance, and he said it was "rustic." You bet!

With our new car, Jean and I would go out to drive-in movies. Being a coupe, it had a shelf even with the top edge of the seats. Carol filled that shelf nicely and most always fell asleep. This arrangement gave us entertainment at a low price. Having this car changed our lives in so many ways. Basically, we were no longer homebound. As I have mentioned before, Jean was able to visit Laura anytime she chose since we had got this car. She was also able to drive to those monthly meetings with her lady friends. How thankful we were to Dave Logan for selling this car to us, especially on such generous terms.

Ups and Downs

I had not dealt openly with the injury I suffered during the Leyte invasion in October 1944, but it was still a problem. Following the doctor's advice concerning the shortness of my right leg, I had all my shoes altered at the time of purchase to help eliminate the limp. I had been to the veterans' hospital and fitted with a back brace, however, the pain was still a daily aggravation that I had to deal with.

We had seen a couple looking at the new house next door. Today, they were back and introduced themselves as the new owners, and they would be moving in soon. Their names were Gladys and John Tucker. They were perhaps in their midfifties, and seemed real friendly. We looked forward to having neighbors.

With the school year approaching, I had been contacted by a member of the Verona school board. They had in mind to begin an evening program, one night per week, during which they would open up the gym in the elementary building to boys aged ten to twelve. They wanted me to sponsor this group. I had agreed to do this. There was no particular agenda other than giving these young boys an evening of fun and fellowship. Basketballs and volleyballs were to be available and the program would begin on the first Monday of September 1948.

In August we were celebrating our first year as homeowners. How blessed we had been to be living here. It had been a year of filling in the gaps between "lack ofs" and "necessities." We had lucked out just before moving in when someone ahead of us on the wait list for a refrigerator cancelled out, which allowed us to be like normal couples who do not have to empty an ice pan under an icebox. Laura and Jean visited back and forth; what a blessing for these sisters who were so far from their Illinois home. As Carol got a bit older, I was sure we would do more socializing with Laura and Frank.

Jean continued her monthly meetings with the young women alumni of Verona High School and was so happy to have those friends. As would happen in a small, close-knit town, most of these women had married local men, so I knew nearly all their husbands. Through Jean I was kept up to date on quite a few of the young people in our community.

My first night with the young boys went well, and they seemed to have had a good time playing basketball. I feared there might be a discipline problem, but everyone was so well mannered that I looked forward to next Monday night. I kept hoping no one would mess with our car while I was in the school, because the doors do not lock and it would be an easy target for pranks.

Today we celebrated our second anniversary in high spirits and in gratitude for the joy that had filled our lives together. How firm was our love for each other and for our daughter, Carol. How wonderful at such a young age to have so much. We truly counted our blessings.

As Jean would turn twenty-three on October 1, we were looking forward to Jim and Jane's wedding on the eighth, and then my birthday on the nineteenth. However, Laura had not been feeling well and had been doctoring with a case of the flu. She had been taken to the hospital, as she was not getting any better. The word from the hospital was shocking. They said she was suffering from peritonitis, a very, very serious situation—life threatening. Mom and Dad were coming in from Glen Ellyn.

Approaching the eighth, Jane and Jim's wedding day, it was evident that Laura's condition was desperate and that they had better get to Pennsylvania immediately. On the evening of the seventh, with a handful of friends and relatives, Jane and Jim were married in the rectory and had flown into Pennsylvania.

Mom and Dad were staying with us. Jane and Jim were staying with his parents here in Verona. The family was spending as much time as possible at the hospital, which was about six miles away, just inside the city limits of Pittsburgh. The diagnosis about Laura's ailment was that she had what was called a "chocolate cyst," which had burst and caused peritonitis. Whether an earlier diagnosis would have helped only God knows, but she was suffering terribly.

Early this morning, Frank called and told us to come to the hospital as soon as possible. Laura was in a coma, with no communication possible. We got there in a hurry and learned that her life was fading fast. Within a couple of hours, Laura passed away. At the age of twenty-seven, newly married and full of hope in her future with Frank, she was taken away from us. Many hopes and plans within our families were dashed. We asked, "Why?" Why did this happen? A question asked since the beginning of time with no real, satisfying answer. As Christians we, in our faith, know that one day God will call us home, not on our schedule, but His. The reality of this life is that we are never quite ready to lose a loved one, or to make that journey ourselves. At the moment we were devastated over Laura's passing, but had to quickly get a grip on things if we were to weather this storm. I read these comforting words: "Precious memories of life can temper the profound sadness of death." How we wish we had more time for memories. She had been so young and vibrant.

The family had a two-day viewing for Laura at a funeral home in Oakmont. Her funeral would be held in Glen Ellyn, Illinois, in a couple of days, depending on her arrival in her hometown. We made ready to drive to Illinois tonight, hoping Carol would sleep most of the way. It was a fourteen-hour drive. My dad was lending us his car for this trip, a 1937 Buick.

As we prepared Dad's car for the trip, he said the car had been using oil during local driving, but might use more on an extended trip, so he put a case of oil (twenty-four quarts) in the trunk. Dad advised me to watch the oil level closely. We had a full load of passengers, with Jim and Jane, Frank's uncle, Carol, Jean, and me.

After travelling seventy-five miles, we stopped to check the oil. It had taken three quarts. Fearful of burning up the engine, we added two quarts every fifty miles. At one stop it was quite windy, and as Jim leaned over to add some oil, the car hood slammed down on his head. There was no serious injury, but he had a headache the rest of the way. We arrived safely, having used twenty-one quarts of oil, an unbelievable consumption for any car. Aside from the oil problem, we had to watch the gas gauge closely, as we had discovered town after town with no filling station opened during the night.

Once we settled in, I called Dad to tell him about the oil problem. He shouted at me, "I told you not to beat that car!" I assured him we had taken every precaution to protect the well-being of his car. He calmed down, apologized, and told me to get another case of oil for the trip home.

Laura's funeral was to be here in Glen Ellyn. I was sure this was not the "homecoming" she had planned. Being so young and so recently a resident, many of her local friends had come to the funeral home in shock over her passing. Dad was devastated over this tragic turn of events. They had been so close. They had ridden the train together every day into Chicago. His nickname for her had been "Mike." For Jean, this was such an overwhelming loss after looking forward to a lifetime with Laura living so close. It was such a blessing to have Carol in our lives to attract our attention. It would be harder on Jean when we got back home when those visits would no longer be a part of her life.

I felt so sorry for Jane and Jim, as their formal wedding had been cancelled and they were unable to have a honeymoon. Hopefully, they could get away for a few days after the funeral. For Mom and Dad, it would be good that the newlyweds would be living with them for the immediate future. For Frank, who could imagine what was on his mind after losing his bride of seven months? They had been so happy in love and marriage.

Following this morning's funeral, we gathered here at the house with each segment of the family thinking, *What is next?* For Jean, Carol, and me, it was getting ready for the trip back to Pennsylvania, with high hopes we would make it with no serious problems with Dad's car. I got extra oil for the trip.

Our return trip was uneventful except for an excessive number of pit stops to add oil. The car used twenty quarts of oil coming home, which made a total of forty-one for the round trip. Dad breathed a sigh of relief when he saw his car back in Pennsylvania. He was going to order all the needed parts to overhaul the engine, so in a few days we would be very involved in that project. I would get a schedule change at the phone company so that I could help. It was just so hard to believe a car could use forty-one quarts of oil in a thousand miles.

Jean was quiet over Laura's passing as we settled in after the trip and funeral. What a blow to their plans to be close together for life. I felt so helpless in comforting Jean in these circumstances, but I was confident in her ability to cope with what had happened. Her strong faith in God would be her refuge.

While things had been in turmoil in our family, the Tuckers had moved in next door. John had been busy in their yard. He was attempting to get some of the "rustic" out of that wall along the driveway. It was so good to have a house and neighbors in place of that unsightly vacant lot. We had good neighbors, and in time we would have an increase, as there were a few vacant lots nearby.

Here in January of a new year, I was meeting weekly with those young boys, fourteen in number. As I got to know them better, it had become a real fun time for me as well as them. I could not ask for a better-behaved group. At the school tonight, Jack Rearick, a friend of many years, showed up and asked if he could be a part of the oversight of these boys. I gladly welcomed the help and shared responsibility. One advantage in teaming with Jack was that in case I could not make it, I knew he would be there.

Having completed two years at my job at the phone company, I was chosen to go to cable splicer's school. As a splicer's helper, I had learned the basics of the job, but one phase I had not touched was handling the hot lead used in wiping joints on the lead sleeves, which were used to enclose the multitudes of wires in a cable splice. Once school was completed, I would be on my own as a splicer with a splicer's helper. This job involved working on aerial cables as well as working underground in manholes. The big value in this job promotion was that there were no hurdles for me to reach top rate in pay grade. It was a time process, but would pay off as a top-paying job.

After two weeks of cable splicer school, I spent a day getting the tools for my job. Each splicer was assigned a small trailer with a full set of tools, a tent for aerial jobs, especially in the rain, and "Men Working" signs. This trailer was moved from site to site and was maintained by a splicer's helper. My helper's name was Buddy Meese, and he seemed like he would be a good teammate. Tomorrow I would start on some aerial work in a new plan of houses, probably the simplest work for a beginner.

Not having a car that would be good for long trips, Jean, Carol, and I flew to Chicago for a vacation, with plans to return by train. We, of course, were staying in Glen Ellyn with Jean's parents, along with Jane and Jim. We hoped to have a better car in the future, which would allow us to drive on our own. We were not involved in anything spectacular, mostly each other's company. Mom had taken Jean and Carol shopping, with purchases for each. So far Mom and Dad had paid for every item of clothing that Carol had since birth. That represented a lot of financial help, for which we were thankful. After a seemingly short vacation, we came back on the train.

The years were passing so quickly. I had just had my third anniversary with the phone company. It seemed like I had just got my new title of cable splicer, but it had been a year. However, I had been offered a chance to go to switchman's school, a venture that would teach me about circuit and relay work and qualify me to hold a job in the central office. That may sound like a desk job, but it was work with the equipment that gave us a dial tone and routed our calls. I accepted the offer, and if I succeeded, my schooling would last several weeks. The wages would be the same as a cable splicer's.

It had been four years since I got out of the Navy, and the only shipmate I had any contact with was Jack Felger. Today I received a letter from Rodger Hennessy, one of our ship's officers during the war. He had scheduled a ship's reunion, here in 1950, in the city of Chicago. That was such good news. We would be able to drive to Illinois, as we had just moved up in the auto world. We had moved from a 1930 Ford Model A coupe to a four-door 1934 Chevrolet. It would be impossible to estimate the value of that Model A to us in the two years we had it. It may have been a bottom-line car, but it brought such joy and convenience at a time when we most needed it. Blessings on Dave Logan for supplying that car.

Earlier in my writings, I mentioned that the state of Pennsylvania was planning to pay a bonus to WWII veterans. I had received a check in the amount of $395. To us, that was a fortune. We were most grateful to the state (taxpayers) who had done this for us.

For several weeks, I had been in school studying to be a switchman. It was like learning another language. I was having a difficult time, but would tough it out. By the way, when Norm Sellers had sent me to the telephone company, he had suggested I ask to be considered for the job of being a switchman. A bit of humor here—my last day as a cable splicer, I worked in a manhole in the middle of the entrance to a cemetery, a "dead end" to my career as a splicer.

Finishing my schooling, I was assigned a job location in the Montrose central office in the East Liberty section of Pittsburgh. This office was about six miles from home with a travel time of twenty minutes each way, which was extremely satisfactory. I found out immediately that much of the equipment I would be working on was so old that it should be in a museum. Also, it was not like the equipment I had studied in school.

Jean and I would be meeting Mamie and Jack at their home in Ohio as we headed for the Navy reunion in Chicago. Neither of us could afford the cost of hotel rooms plus three meals a day in Chicago restaurants, so we would be staying with Mom and Dad Simpson in Glen Ellyn. Jane and Jim had moved into their own home, so there would be plenty of room for us. Also, Mom would care for Carol each day we attended the reunion.

It was so good to see our former shipmates and their wives. So far there were fourteen of the crew from near and far. Most of our time had been spent visiting with each other and planning to continue meeting in the future. Last night we attended the stage production of *Mr. Roberts*, a Navy-based show with so many wonderful spots depicting some of the things we had experienced on board our ship, presented in very humorous ways. We thoroughly enjoyed the show. A collection was taken for postage and other materials for mailings on another reunion and given to a man who said he would set up the next reunion. After three days, we broke up and left for our homes. I am happy to report that our '34 Chevy performed beautifully on the round trip.

All was going well with my new job, and we were pretty well settled in for the fall season. Jean and I were ready for our October birthdays. Jean had an appointment with Dr. Aronson and announced she was now pregnant with our second child, with an expected delivery date near May 1, 1951. Jean's twin sister was expecting her first child about two weeks later.

Speaking of babies, our baby, Carol, was no longer a baby, but a happy young girl who would be three years old next month (November 13, 1950). She was strong and healthy and had a playmate, Barbara Richey, who lived two doors away. Barbara was a year older than Carol. Her parents and I had been neighborhood friends while growing up.

With a new baby due in two months and a plan to go to Glen Ellyn for Thanksgiving, we thought it wise to get a car with an automatic transmission. Jean was doing well in her pregnancy, but shifting gears in our old Chevy was getting to be a bit of a problem. We purchased a 1946 Nash. At five years of age, it should be a great improvement on a trip. The Chevy made two round trips to Chicago without any problems, for which we were grateful. We were anxiously looking forward to the our baby's arrival. Jean looked so beautiful. I loved her so.

Through the pages of this book, I have often noted my belief that a Silent Partner was so close and mysteriously "opening doors" for me in a timely way. I had sensed his presence in so many instances over a period of years. Now, that other presence was leaning on me to become a Christian minister. I had never discussed this with anybody until recently, when I told Jean what was happening. I was active in my church, but by no means was I a leader. I must confess that in the face of the many blessings showered upon me, I had felt undeserving, and likewise, I felt unqualified to answer this call. Further, I had no formal training, nor education beyond high school. I felt I was on a guilt trip for not saying yes, because I was looking harder for excuses. I felt a need to share this burden with my readers.

Jean had done a remarkable job of coping with Laura's passing. The timing of her pregnancy may have had something to do with her tranquil demeanor. She was excited as we neared the end of April, as our baby could come anytime during the last week or the first week in May. Mom Simpson planned to be here around the arrival time. I hoped she predicted well, as she would be caring for Carol until Jean and baby got home from the hospital. We had not yet chosen a name.

Mom had arrived from Glen Ellyn on the twenty-eighth, praise God. During the night, Jean's water broke and we rushed her to the hospital, where she delivered a baby girl almost immediately. The date was May 1, 1951. It was a perfect delivery, and all was well as Mom and I talked with Dr. Aronson by the nursery. He was ecstatic, as this was the first baby he had ever delivered on his own birthday. In the middle of our joy, a nurse came up to Dr. Aronson expressing concern about our baby's breathing. With that, they brought her out of the nursery on a cart. We got only a momentary glimpse of her as she was rolled into the emergency room. We were informed that she had a lung problem and that a team of doctors were working on her. Mom and I were in shock over what had just happened, so we went to Jean's room and told her what was going on. She, of course, was upset, but was in her usual patient state, as she was never one to panic. As the day wore on, we stayed with Jean and were kept posted about what was going on. Having been here till late day, we were going home for the night. I loved her so very much.

The phone rang early this morning. It was a call from the hospital, asking me to come right away. Upon my arrival, I was informed that our daughter had died. Wow! What a blast! How do we handle this? How do *I* handle this? What do I say to Jean? She was just recovering from Laura's passing, and now this. Dr. Aronson appeared and was so saddened by this turn of events. He went in to see Jean and explained to her what had happened. To the doctor, in her own stoical way, she said, "Don't worry about it, I'll be back." Jean never ceases to amaze me how she handles hurt. I wish I had her strength. As I visited Jean, in hopes of comforting her, I was overwhelmed by her composure. She wanted to go home to Carol and get on with things. I had to leave her, as I had to arrange for our baby's funeral.

I was not ready for what had just happened to our baby. Trying to sort out what to do was like trying to climb a wall leaning toward me. We, of course, had no insurance, no gravesite, and no money. Dad and I talked about what to do, and he told me he would set things up with a funeral director. Along with our pastor, Bill Daugherty, Mom Simpson, my parents, and myself, we gathered at the cemetery for burial. The burial was in an area of unmarked graves for infants. It was my only answer to an overwhelming situation. I was grateful that we at least had a Christian burial service, with regrets of not being able to do more.

Jean was released from the hospital in three days, and we were trying to get back to normal. Mom wanted to get back to Glen Ellyn as soon as possible in case Jane's baby came early. She was due in less than two weeks. We took Mom to the train station for her trip back to Chicago.

It was so good to have Mom here for a few days to help Jean in many ways, but also to look after Carol while Jean regained her strength. Our plans for an enlarged family had been sidetracked, but by God's grace we would have other opportunities. I would rely on Jean's promise to the doctor about "coming back."

We got word this evening from Mom that Jane had given birth to a baby girl today. They named her Ellen, and she was the first grandchild in the Beers family. She was strong and healthy at the moment, and we prayed that all would continue so. Mom would be there to help; we had kept her busy. This was May 13, so Ellen's birth was right on schedule.

Having made it through the summer of '51, we saw Carol growing and having a good time with her playmate, Barbara Richey. Jean was doing well and we were packing for a trip to Glen Ellyn for Thanksgiving. I did not relish this long drive, but it was the most economical way for us to travel. We drove all night, spelling each other at the wheel. Snow was a slight problem through Indiana, where we slid off the road into the grassy median strip and were fortunate to get back onto the road without help.

During our first night here at the Simpsons', I awoke at 3:30 a.m. with a severe pain in my right side. The family doctor was summoned, and his opinion was that it was an appendix problem. I was rushed to the hospital. I was examined upon arrival and told I would be operated on very shortly to have my appendix removed. About a half hour later, the doctor returned with a colleague telling me he had second thoughts about the operation because I was not doubled up in pain but lying out straight, and that I might be having a kidney stone attack. His second thought was correct, and I did indeed pass a stone. I have never had such pain in my life. I was quite thankful I did not have an appendix operation, and I never want to have such pain again. I was released from the hospital, but not soon enough to attend the family Thanksgiving dinner. The hospital was in Elmhurst, Illinois. The rest of our vacation was uneventful and we returned home safely. Also, we got to see Ellen, our first niece.

Our '46 Nash began to have some undercarriage problems where some welding needed to be done. After the repairs were completed, the car worked fine, but I could see the problem occurring again, so we talked about getting another car. We had purchased our car at a Nash dealer, so we returned there to make a deal on a 1952 brand-new Nash. Wow, had we come up in the world! But now the payments. At least we should not have any repairs or tires to buy for a while.

I have not mentioned much about my siblings. They were doing well. My sister, Audrey, graduated from Slippery Rock State Teachers College with a degree in physical education and now taught this subject in high school. Brother Bud finished two years at Slippery Rock and then spent four years at the University of Pittsburgh, graduating from their dental school. He had his dental office here in Verona and took good care of our teeth, for which we were grateful. He and Hap recently had their first child, Susan, born on January 20, 1953, which happens to be the date of our Dad's fiftieth birthday. Susan and Dad would always be able to celebrate together. Dad was so happy over her birth.

We just received some of the most shocking news in our married life. Our daughter Carol's closest friend and playmate, Barbara Richey, had been diagnosed with polio. She was now in the Watson Home for crippled children, as she was paralyzed in her legs. We, of course, were in a panic over this tragic news and were having Dr. Aronson keep a check on Carol. So far, Carol showed no sign of any polio symptoms—thank God! I was reminded of my friend and shipmate, Jack Felger, whose brother and sister both died of polio.

We needed a change in the news, and some came today. Jane and Jim were expecting their second child near the end of March 1954. More good news—double good news—Jean told me she thought she was pregnant. She was going to make an appointment with Dr. Aronson.

The Tuckers, our next-door neighbors, had had their home up for sale for the past month and had a buyer. They had not been here long and had told me they wanted to live out in the country. They were moving to West Sunbury, a place I had never heard of, but it was here in western Pennsylvania.

With Carol starting school in October, it seemed wise to get a used car for Jean to drive her in her first year. Shannon Road was no place for Jean or Carol to walk. A friend here in Verona was giving up driving and had sold me his 1938 Plymouth coupe for sixty dollars. It needed a new clutch, which Dad and I would replace. We could not buy cheaper reliable transportation.

Moving On

The Tuckers had moved out and a new family had moved in. Their name was Dreher—Bill, Fran, and Nancy. Nancy was a year younger than Carol and would probably become her new playmate in Barbara's absence, whose condition was not improving. The Drehers were a bit older than us. We looked forward to a good relationship.

Jean had her visit with Dr. Aronson, and he confirmed she was pregnant, with an expected birth date in late April 1954. That would be about a month after sister Jane delivered. We were so happy over the news of both pregnancies. We prayed all would go well in both cases. I had never mentioned how fresh and neat Jean was about herself and our home. She was so special, and I loved her so dearly. I was so blessed to have her as my wife.

After four months in first grade, Carol was really happy in school, we were glad she had some time in kindergarten at our church. However, her teacher, Mrs. Cleland, had told us she believed Carol needed glasses. We followed up on her advice and had her fitted right away. Carol missed Barbara, her playmate. Barbara was in intensive therapy for her polio.

We had lived in this home six and a half years and had been blessed to be homeowners. We loved this home, but found that getting Carol to school on snowy days was a bit chancy. There was a contractor surveying and staking out some large acreage near the school, so we were contemplating choosing a home in that plan. We decided to take the first step by picking a site early so as to have the best choice. It was a case of envisioning your new neighborhood as we stood in the middle of a forest with a salesman with a plot plan. We wanted an elevated corner lot. The new street in this plan had a sharp curve in it. The inside of the curve was elevated with a good view of the Allegheny River down in the valley. We chose that spot as the site for our future home, and at a later date would choose what style of a home to build. Jean loved two-story colonials . . . I wondered what our choice would be.

Today, April 4, 1954, Mom Simpson called with the news that sister Jane had given birth to a healthy baby girl this morning. They named her Donna. Along with Ellen, they were now a family of four. It was our hope to be a family of four within a month; Jean looked almost ready to deliver, and she looked so beautiful.

We met with an agent about the style of home we wanted to build. All the homes would be built by the Calvin Crawford Company and would be completed in early 1955. Surprisingly, we chose a two-story colonial red brick with the upper half of the front finished with white clapboard, which would protrude a foot past the brick. I would build all the kitchen cabinets, including the sink units. For extra special wiring, I had to contract with the electrician. Later in the year, we would put our present home on the market for sale. My parents had also made a contract to buy one of these new homes. They would be two blocks away on the main road near the bus line.

The month of April has rolled by rather quickly, and with it a bit of excitement here at the end. At 11:00 p.m. last night, Jean suddenly went into labor. She was having severe pains, and I was afraid she was going to give birth before I could get her into the car. Our '52 Nash had a front seat that folded back to a level position. With Jean lying out flat, I drove as fast as I could into the city toward the Montefiore Hospital. Jean was hollering that the baby was coming. At that moment, we pulled alongside of a parked city police car with two officers in it. I shouted to them that Jean was about to deliver and we had to get to the Montefiore Hospital. The driver shouted, "Follow us!" They turned on their flashing lights and gave a high-speed run to the hospital with their siren blaring loudly. The police alerted people at the emergency room that Jean was outside in the car. They rushed her inside, where she delivered a baby boy at 12:30 a.m. I was in such a panic that the officers wanted to know if this was our first child. We had decided that if we had a boy, we would name him Robert Warren—Robert after my Uncle Bob, and Warren after Jean's dad. Jean and Robert came through this exciting drama with flying colors. The new daddy survived on shaky legs.

The delivery time was 12:30 a.m., April 30, 1954, but when we got Robert's birth certificate it read 11:30 p.m., April 29, 1954. I challenged the hospital about this recorded time because it changed our son's birth date. They informed me that although he was born on daylight saving time, they had to record his birth on standard time.

Here, in the middle of summer, the contractor had removed all the trees where they planned to build the new homes. They had rough graded where the streets would be. Foundations for each home were begun at the start of our street. Our home would be the eleventh house along the street. With great anxiety, I visited the site every evening. One evening this week on my visit I found that they had dug out the foundation for our home, and the driveway had been dug out on the opposite side from where we wanted it. When I contacted the construction supervisor about this, he told me the contractor said our driveway would have been too close to the curve in the street. They were going to reverse the layout of the house, meaning our kitchen window would have a closeup view of the house next door instead of our side yard. I convinced them that the driveway being too close to the curve was my concern, so they dug a new driveway. I would continue to monitor what they were doing.

Jean was kept so busy with Robert, whom we had already begun to call "Bobby." Once Carol was off to school, Jean's routine of being the world's best homemaker began—you know, "a place for everything and everything in its place." Her friends teased her about her "neatness attitude," but I loved it.

Progress on our new home was coming along well. The block foundation had been completed and framing was up to the second-story level. In a few days, it should be under roof. After that, progress would slow to a walk as the various tradesmen each performed their specialty.

We faced a problem concerning my parents' new home, as progress was lagging in its construction. Our master plan was to get our present home sold, move up Shannon Road, and live temporarily in Mom and Dad's vacated house. We put a one-dollar ad in the local paper advertising our home for sale at $12,900. An elderly couple came to look at it and said that it was nice as they left. No one else came to look, so we placed another one-dollar ad in the local paper. Immediately, we got a phone call from the elderly couple, Mr. and Mrs. Peterson. Mr. Peterson said, "Take your house off the market. We are going to buy it right away." We met with them, and they said they would like us to reduce the price to $12,750 and throw in our beautiful burgundy living room rug. We agreed, and they paid cash for our home and wanted us out in thirty days.

My parents were not too happy. I did not blame them, but we were doubling up with them for three weeks until their home was finished. Here we were with two children and a German shepherd moving in on Mom and Dad. We were not happy about it. No one had expected their new-home completion to be delayed. We could not afford to bicker over the great deal we made in selling our home. Can you imagine, selling it at a cost of two dollars in ad money? We did not bring any furniture to Mom and Dad's. The Petersons allowed us to store our furniture in their basement. We had been so blessed.

Under the circumstances, here at Mom and Dad's, we thought it would be good if Jean, Carol, and Bobby went out to Glen Ellyn for several days, including Christmas Day. They went by plane, and I missed them very much. It was not in our plan, but tomorrow was Christmas Eve and I just had to go to Glen Ellyn. I rushed into Pittsburgh and got a round-trip train ticket to Chicago, arriving Christmas morning. I made good connections on the electric train out to Glen Ellyn and got there before they served Christmas dinner. It was such a joyous reunion with my family, my depression was cured immediately. I returned home by train. Jean and our children would be home before New Year's.

Mom and Dad's home was finished and they moved out. My friend and coworker, Jimmy Joe Maddy, and I moved our furniture up from the Petersons. We were not setting up anything in a permanent way, as we would be moving to our new home within a month. At least we were able to bring Pal, our German shepherd, into the house. He had been in a pen in the backyard for three weeks. Pal was used to living indoors and was quite happy to get out of that pen.

Work on our new home was progressing rather slowly at the moment due to the winter weather. We expected to move into our home in mid-February, but the time had been moved back to the end of the month. A major problem was that they could not plaster when the temperature was below freezing.

We got rid of our second car ('38 Plymouth) when we moved into my parents' home, as we were much closer to Carol's school. Later this week we would be moving. Today, Jean needed our car, so she came to my office to bring me home. When I got in the car, she told me she had taken Pal out in the yard just before leaving home, and he had run away. I told her we would look for him when we got home. As we neared the house, I could see Pal lying dead on the berm of the road. I did not say anything until we were inside, because I knew what the emotional response would be for Jean and Carol. I gathered Pal's remains and buried him. It was so sad here, as we loved him so very much. Bobby did not understand what happened. So many times as Bobby sat in his stroller, Pal would come by and lick him on the forehead.

Well, today was moving day, February 28, 1955, with two of my best friends and coworkers, Jimmy Joe Maddy and Tom Fritz, working with me loading and unloading a rented stake-body truck. It was only three blocks to our new home, so we had no need to try to do it in one load. There was no landscaping, so we were saving a lot of steps by backing the truck up to the back door to unload. With the help of my friends, we did a good job of having everything in its proper place, such as having the beds put together.

The kitchen cabinets were in place, but without doors, as there had not been enough time to finish them. That project would be even further behind had I not had the help of Jimmy Joe. Moving so soon after Pal's death had aided in coping with his loss, but we were all so sad about what had happened. All went well in the move, and in this case, we had electricity and a toilet seat. Who could ask for anything more?

As time passed, Jean and I had become more active in our church. Jean taught Sunday school in a "team-teaching" setup with Elsie Madine. They had a large class of fifth and sixth graders. Jean just loved doing this. After three years working with those young boys in the Verona school, I gave it up, as other demands took up so much of my time. In the church, I had held numerous offices along with ushering in the Sunday morning worship services. I still felt the Spirit nipping at my heels, calling me into His service, but so far I kept sidestepping the issue. Jean and I continued discussing this call and that maybe my inaction would send a message.

Having made a profit on the sale of our first home, we had the funds to carpet our new home and have venetian shades installed on all the windows. We also purchased drapes and had installed many extra electrical outlets. There was money to pave our driveway and put in concrete walks. With help, I would do all this work. Maybe I should have been a contractor. I loved construction work. Until the last frost, locally, the contractor was not allowed to finish paving our street. The grading had been completed and all the base for paving was in place. However, a slurry of mud had accumulated over this base, and it tracked into every conceivable place. Yuck!

After getting final clearance for finishing our street, the paving equipment had come and gone, and we now had a beautiful street and "cleaner carpeting." Once the street was paved, I had our driveway graded in line with the curb edge. With help, I got the driveway paved with concrete. I graded our yard and had a real nice lawn growing, way ahead of any other property on the street. My progress in getting so much done so quickly was rewarded in having our home pictured in a publication called *American Home*. This is good for my ego, but better for the contractor who got some free publicity, as he was listed as the builder.

This kept happening: we got word from Mom that Jane and Jim were expecting their third child in mid-October 1955. It seemed like only yesterday that Jim had accompanied us on that New Year's weekend when he met Jane. They may have to get a bigger house.

Today, April 29, was Bobby's first birthday. He was growing big and was quite healthy. This young boy had lived in three different houses during his first year of life. I hoped Bobby was in manhood before he moved again. Bobby kept Jean busy; he was so active. I had to get busy in the backyard, as my plan was to put up a swing set, a sliding board, and a sandbox. Carol would probably use everything but the sandbox. She had found a new playmate in Candi Swisher, who lived across the street. All the new homes in our neighborhood were now occupied with families much like ourselves in age and family content. My cousin, Pat, Uncle Bob's daughter, with her husband, Miles Humphrey, lived three doors away. Miles worked for the Bell Telephone Company as I did. When he had returned from the Korean War, I had urged him to put in an application for employment, much as Norm Sellers had urged me to do. I mentioned that Carol had a new playmate. The update on her former playmate, Barbara Richey, was that she was now living at home and was severely crippled in both legs.

How quickly we had moved through the year into October with Jean and I reaching our thirtieth birthdays. We had first written to each other at the age of nineteen. Speaking of birthdays, Mom called to tell us that Jane had given birth yesterday, October 22, 1955, to a baby boy, who had been named David. It was good that Jim had gotten in with the phone company to support their growing family.

Time marches on. As I mentioned above, the year 1955 went by so rapidly for us because we were so busy moving into this new home with all its associated demands. We did well and were quite comfortable and blessed to be in these new surroundings. In the midst of this fast-moving life, today we paused to celebrate our tenth anniversary, September 14, 1956. I knew how deeply in love we were with each other, but found it so hard to put into words the depth of my love for Jean. I knew, with my whole heart, that my life would never be complete without Jean at my side. She was the essence of love, and I had fed on that love every day since the day she had come into my life. In the New Testament, 1 Corinthians 13:13, we read that "there are three things which last forever, faith, hope and love, but the greatest of them all is love." My love for Jean was first, but in her I had faith, hope, and love. She was the snow on a white-capped mountain, pure and divine. Yes, this was our tenth anniversary, and only God knew if we should have another, but for me every day was an anniversary.

In our age group, growing a family seemed to be the norm. My brother, Bud, and his wife, Hap, had added a son, Paul, to their family here on June 26, 1957. They were now a family of four. Bud had done well in establishing his dental practice and had recently moved to a new location in a building he had purchased. Hap was a schoolteacher.

My sister, Audrey, and her fiancée, Dick Davis, had announced their plans to be married on July 26, 1958, just six months away. Our cousin Delbert Remaley, a Methodist minister, was going to perform the wedding ceremony in his church, which was about eighty miles away in the town of Dubois, Pennsylvania. Jean and I would be attending the wedding with our children, after which we would go a little farther north into Canada for a brief vacation.

It had not been my habit to report on our trips to and from Illinois or on Jean's parents' visits to us. These were routine family visits, which were accomplished, on average, twice yearly. Jane and Jim were in a like situation, with Jim's parents living here in Verona. We all kept in close touch with one another and had the very best of relationships. So far this year we had gone to Glen Ellyn twice, and after Audrey and Dick's wedding tomorrow, we would have yet another trip, the aforementioned, into Canada.

We were gathered here today in Dubois for the wedding. With Dick's family and ours, we were probably, in number, thirty-five to forty people. As the ceremony progressed, a sense of the Holy Spirit came over me. In past writings, I have mentioned these encounters and had chosen to remain uninterested, feeling so unqualified for the ministry. Well, here on July 26, 1958, I said yes to the call. Through the remainder of the ceremony and the wedding reception, I did not speak of what had happened.

We left Dubois after the celebration and were heading toward Canada as I began telling Jean about my decision. She seemed not too surprised at what I was telling her, and we began discussing what to do about pursuing "the call." I did not wish to go public about this, so we decided to get started in a private way through cousin Delbert. We returned home from Canada and made arrangements to meet with Delbert in their parsonage, spending the night with him and Leatha. He told me I would have to go through four years of college and three years of seminary, but I should approach the district superintendent in the Methodist church in the area where I live before striking out on my own. A superintendent was over all pastors in a geographic area.

I must digress. When I was about twelve years of age, there had been a young man working in a family grocery store in our neighborhood. This young man had finished college and was working there in the summer when I heard he was going to go to seminary to become a preacher. This was during the Great Depression, and I found it hard to believe he would give up that good job in the store to become a preacher. Well, as it turned out, the district superintendent I approached about my future as a minister was the man who gave up that job to become a preacher. What a small world!

The program he discussed with me involved the study and examination on a set number of books, which if successfully completed, would qualify me for a license to preach. The next step would be to enter college, and with this license to preach, serve as student minister in as many as three country churches on weekends. A parsonage would be provided for me and my family, with a yearly income and car expense. After four years of college, three years of seminary would be required. Upon graduation, I would be ordained as an elder in the Methodist church, qualified to serve full time as a minister under a bishop's appointment.

I agreed to enlist in this difficult program. Jean was at my side as I went through the studies for a license to preach. I took the college entrance exams at Clarion State Teachers College in Clarion, Pennsylvania, and was accepted. It was then up to the Clarion district superintendent to line up a parish in which I would pastor during four years at college. Dr. Heitzenrater, the district superintendent, put together a three-point circuit (three churches) in which I would be serving. This had all taken a year, and I would be entering college this fall (1959). Jean had supported me throughout this year, and I was well aware that for all my good intentions, there was a chance I could fail. Therefore, I owed it to Jean, Carol, and Bobby to cover us all with a year's leave of absence from the phone company where I had been employed for more than twelve years. Thus, I had applied for this leave and waited anxiously for a reply.

I had just been hit in the pit of my stomach. The company's reply to my request was, "No, we do not have a need for a preacher." In a year of study, I would not receive one word of learning toward becoming a preacher, especially in a state college. I was so shaken by this news that I had taken a week's vacation to *think*!

In my life, the Lord had opened and closed many doors. Some of opportunity had opened, and some preventing failure had closed. Did I accept this closed door as a blessing or a failure? Was I short on faith? Was this roadblock perhaps a weigh station, a moment to weigh my options? Throughout the pages of this book, the Lord had abundantly blessed me without seeking a decision from my side. Likewise, he had delivered me from critical situations, even death during the war. I had said yes to the Holy Spirit, but was now in the midst of shattered plans. I must not surrender because someone said no. It has been said many times, "Nothing ventured, nothing gained." In weighing my options, I decided to return to square one and go back to the district superintendent who had set my original course. I had accepted the fact that the "no" I received might, in reality, be the Lord's doing.

My first duty had to be a call to Doctor Heitzenrater, informing him of my situation. He spent a lot of time with me setting up that three-point circuit. I know I had let him down. A message to the college was very important at the moment. I had worked hard during this past year and prayed all was not lost.

I approached my area district superintendent for the second time, informing him of what had happened. He shared my disappointment and explained there was another way that led to ordination. If I were judged to be a mature person, had had meaningful life experiences, had a reliable résumé, and had the recommendation of my local church's governing body, I could enter a "course of study" leading to ordination. That was a lot to chew, but it was a way. With the books I studied for my license to preach, plus the ones in this course of study, it would total more than fifty-five. I had to study each book, take a written exam, and mail the answer sheet to a seminary professor for grading. All answers had to be typed up in a strict format. As I was the person who, upon graduating from high school, had said, "I will never open another book," I would be eating a lot of crow. I had committed myself to enter this course of study. My guess was that it would take six and a half years to finish.

I had begun to accumulate the books assigned to this course, which were purchased through the Methodist bookstore in Pittsburgh. There would be a considerable cost involved. However, as a student, I received a small discount. I have extolled the wonderful qualities that define my wife, Jean, and now I must add another, for she was typing all my worksheet answers for mailing. This was no easy task, for she ended up correcting my spelling while deciphering my writing. I was so blessed to have Jean as a life partner. She was so easy to love.

As we moved through 1959, I found myself extremely busy as a full-time employee at the phone company, a family man, and a student. I was a long way from mastering good study habits.

There did not seem to be enough hours in the day. Now, cousin Delbert had asked me to preach in his church in two weeks, on the eighteenth of October. As you know, I had never preached nor prepared a sermon, but the Spirit would not allow me to turn down this opportunity. I was so nervous, but I had to face this test if I was one day going to be ordained into the ministry.

I had chosen a fitting title for my first sermon: "You Have Been Called." My call into the ministry was not answered for several years, but this call from Delbert demanded a quick answer. I knew in my heart I had to say yes. This call had taken me away from my studies, as I had to compose a message, but I guessed that was "part of the whole" in ministry. On July 26 last year, in Delbert's church in Dubois, I had answered the call, but his newly assigned church was in Reynoldsville, Pennsylvania, this time.

Well, I prepared my sermon and delivered it in the Reynoldsville Church this past Sunday. Though nervous, things went well and I was much relieved it was over with. Now back to my studies. However, my home church, Rosedale Methodist, had invited me to preach the first Sunday of the new year. I had a sense of being "initiated" into the ministry. I cannot help recalling how I refused the nomination to run for president of my senior class in high school, because if I had won, I would have had to deliver a speech at graduation. I was a happy vice president.

The governing body of my local church decided that since I was licensed to preach and that I had preached that first Sunday of this year, it would be helpful if I would agree to become their assistant pastor. This was an honor for me, and so I agreed to do this without pay, but accepted their offer to buy my books for my course of study. Filling in while the head pastor was away might be all I could offer due to my other commitments, but it was an opportunity to get the feel of things. With Jean teaching Sunday school and Carol and Bobby attending class, we had become a very involved family.

All work and no play could be boring, so I allowed myself to get interested in rooting for the Pittsburgh Pirates 1960 baseball team. Over the years, the Pirates had been the "champions of futility" in many of their seasons, but this team rose to the top and played in the World Series against the mighty New York Yankees. In a series where the Yankees outscored the Pirates in embarrassing numbers, they were still able to beat the Yankees three times, taking the series into a seventh and final game played here in Pittsburgh. With the seventh game tied nine to nine in the bottom of the ninth inning, Bill Mazeroski came to bat as the leadoff hitter and promptly drove the ball over the left field wall for the game-winning home run. The crowd went wild, as did the city of Pittsburgh, for the mighty Yankees had been vanquished. I was a little excited also, as I had been there!

Beyond the Fifties

For the ninth time, in these writings, I am able to announce the birth of another child. My sister-in-law, Hap, gave birth on this thirteenth day of March 1961 to a girl named Becky. Bud and Hap now had three children. Jim and Jane also had three children, while Jean and I had two, having lost another one in her second day of life.

As I go through page after page in this book, I look back on why I am doing this. Certainly I am not an accomplished author. So many things have happened in this journey of mine that I began relating them to others in casual conversations. Time after time people said, "Why don't you write a book?" or "You should write a book." At this point, you can see that I have taken them seriously. Many of the recent pages have covered things far afield from the stories that triggered these writings. For a change of pace, I have decided to relate a few stories from outside my family.

Early in my Navy career, I related my time at diesel school at Navy Pier in Chicago, Illinois. One evening, some of my fellow students and I went to a restaurant in the city. I have mentioned how wonderful their citizenry was at treating servicemen and women. While at this restaurant, a woman came over to our table and greeted us, then wanted to know where our hometowns were. When I told her I was from Verona, Pennsylvania, she quickly replied that she had been raised in Pennsylvania. She said she was from Somerset. I told her I used to go to a small town near there to visit my cousin, a place called Rockwood.

"Well," she said, "that is really where I lived. What is your cousin's name?" I had only mentioned his last name when she shouted, "Bob

Bitner, I used to date him!" Then she hollered over to husband that I was Bob Bitner's cousin. What a small world!

Over the years, we visited one of my former shipmates in Crystal City, Missouri—Lee White, and his wife, Mildred. Lee's parents lived nearby and were quite active for people in their midnineties. Lee's dad drove an old Rambler automobile. He was nervous over his dad's driving habits and begged him to give up driving, but without success. One day his dad called him and told him he had decided to give up driving.

"Praise God, Dad, I am so happy and thankful for your decision."

Then came a reply from Mr. White: "By the way, Lee, I drove through the Smiths' garage today."

"Oh, Dad, was anyone hurt?"

"Just my Rambler, son, just my Rambler."

Andy Ottinger, another former shipmate, visited us some years after the war with his family. He related an incident that happened on the boardwalk in Atlantic City, New Jersey. In the crowd that day their youngest son got lost. In near panic, the family divided up and began to look for him. As Andy waded through the crowd, he saw a policeman coming toward him with the lost son in his grip. Double joy—the lost was found, and the police officer was Larry Renze, another one of our wartime shipmates. What a small world! What a wonderful world!

The beat goes on. I was still knee deep in my studies and other church activities. For example, I managed our church basketball team in a YMCA church league. I was careful to not claim that I was a coach, for that talent has evaded me. Sports has always been an interest of mine, as I played both football and basketball in high school. At one stretch, our church team had won thirty-six games in a row before losing in overtime to the Verona Presbyterian team. We had just concluded our 1961–62 season.

I thought it was all over, but here was the latest news: Jean's twin sister, Jane, had just delivered a baby girl, named Julie. She had come into this world more than six years after brother David's birth. I believed Jim and Jane would be spoiling this latest child, born on February 6, 1962.

It had been a blessing to me to have been the assistant pastor here at Rosedale Methodist Church. Since they had first invited me to hold this post, I had been privileged to preach sixteen times. That was a lot while maintaining my studies. Speaking of my studies, I had recently spent several weeks on one of my study books. I read the book and the associated questions I was expected to answer, but was totally lost in being unable to understand any of it. I desperately needed class study, but that was not to be. Jean and I pored over this situation until I took the bull by the horns, sitting down and racking my brains for an answer one question at a time. Finally, the exam was completed, and I must confess—I not only did not understand the book, but the answers did not make sense to me. However, Jean typed it all up and mailed it in for grading, expecting my first failing grade. An undue amount of time passed without a response from the seminary. Then one day Jean called me at the office to inform me that the results had come back. I feared what she was about to tell me.

"You got an A on your exam, and the grader suggests that you consider full-time formal study," she told me. Wow! I was overwhelmed and pleased at her report, and we both had a good laugh over it and wondered if the grader really understood my answers. All is well that ends well!

Having closed out the 1962–63 basketball season in the YMCA church league, I kept myself quite busy in ministry and study. Through this month of May, I had been averaging at least one preaching assignment each month since the beginning of the year. In addition, I was called upon to conduct a funeral. This was new territory for me, so I called another pastor for advice, as our head pastor was on vacation. Well advised, I handled the funeral as best I could as a rookie. A few days later, I presided over a second funeral, as our pastor was still away. I was beginning to get the hang of it, but I would be happy to see Pastor Bob back from vacation. Last year I had to do two weddings in his absence, my first and second. Still working full time at the phone company, I was pressed for time to get my studies up to date. I needed more time to be a husband and father; Jean had been so supportive while keeping our household in order.

I received a call from Dr. Sproule Boyd, the district superintendent in our district of the Methodist church. He wanted to have a meeting with me in his office. This seemed strange, but I went to his office. He began by telling me about a small group of people who were meeting in a fire hall for worship with a college student leading them. This student would be returning to college in mid-September. I knew what was coming.

He asked, "Would you be willing to go there and be their pastor?"

Having been called to preach, how could I say anything but yes? Dr. Boyd explained that this mission would be under the wing of First Methodist Church in McKeesport and that I would be associate pastor of that church. Mrs. Nellie Jones (a church staff member), Dr. Boyd, and I held a meeting to familiarize me with what I was expected to do. They also acquainted me with the Green Valley fire hall and gave me a key. I met with Mr. Dean Byrom, the college student in question. He refreshed me on the procedures he had been following during the past weeks and informed me that his last Sunday would be September 15, 1963.

Jean and I, along with our children, Carol and Bob, appeared at the fire hall on Sunday, September 22, for my first service. We met some of the early arrivals before the service began and were warmly received. The title of my first message was "Spiritual Workers for the Spiritual Harvest." It seemed appropriate for the task ahead of us. There were about thirty-five people in attendance. We saw an immediate need for bulletins for each Sunday service, so Jean and I purchased a well-used mimeograph, stencils, and ink. On our second Sunday at Green Valley, the congregation was highly pleased to have official programs in their hands. Jean did all the typing and copy work, as she had much office experience prior to our marriage. Also, she still kept busy typing all my seminary work. Jean was helping to organize a Sunday school program and was teaching a class. We were all thrilled to have fifty people in attendance.

The first Sunday in October was Worldwide Communion Sunday, so it was very meaningful for me to serve communion on my own for the first time. We needed to get a kneeler for this service, because it would be more meaningful in a kneeling position. We also needed a pulpit, which I was in the process of fashioning from an old television console, to which I would add a light.

This new assignment as "head pastor," my studies toward ordination, and working full time at the phone company were rather overwhelming me, as there were not enough hours in the day. I had to make a drastic change in my hourly schedule. To find extra time, I had begun arriving at my office at 6:00 a.m., two hours before starting time. In these two hours before my telephone work began, I was able to work on my studies or my sermons. The quiet in these hours was a greater bonus than I had ever dreamed, as my hourly production was greatly enhanced. In addition to the previously mentioned items that consumed my time, I visited my parish on my day off, knocking on doors in an effort to enlarge our congregation. I had been visiting those of our number who were hospitalized. My wife and our children were making an immeasurable sacrifice, as our time together had diminished since my appointment at Green Valley. My ministry was indeed a co-ministry, as Jean was constantly contributing to the whole of it all. How blessed I was to be married to this angel.

On October 27, I delivered a message entitled "Everybody Can Tell Somebody," with the idea that we needed to reach out to this whole community and let it be known that we were here to serve our Lord Jesus Christ. Our numbers were growing, and the spirit of this congregation was contagious. This growth was noted with enthusiasm by Dr. Boyd and his wife the following Sunday as they slipped in unannounced. I suspected that the good doctor wanted to witness how I was doing. Too bad he did not come the following week, as we had reached a milestone with one hundred in attendance.

Tragedy struck at the heart of our nation this past week as the president of the United States, John F. Kennedy, was assassinated in Dallas, Texas. It was a somber Sunday morning. I chose not to preach on the tragedy, but observed a moment of silence and offered a special prayer. The solemnity of this occasion swelled our attendance on November 24, 1963, to 125. I was very thankful for the phenomenal growth in our congregation during these first two months.

We were so blessed to have the use of this wonderful building. Our heartfelt thanks went out to all the Green Valley firemen who had been so generous toward our mission in this community. Some of them were members of our congregation. We were the only church in this area. We held our first Christmas Eve service with a standing-room-only crowd of 155. These numbers were encouraging to us, and the talk was not about *if* we would become a legal congregation, but *when*. Our goal was to be officially organized this year, because we would soon need a building of our own, which would take years to achieve. We had to be patient as a congregation, much as I had been patient during these years of studies toward my ordination.

Along the way, I finished the pulpit I had been constructing, and we acquired a portable kneeler for communion from another group who was moving into a new church building. These items had given us a more organized look in setting up our worship center each Sunday morning. There was a gentleman in our congregation, Mr. Curwen Colflesh, who agreed to assist me in the communion service, which enhanced the beauty of this special service. I was grateful for his help and his devotion.

I talked with Dr. Boyd about taking the steps toward formalizing our group of worshipers as a bona fide Methodist congregation. While many of our group had backgrounds in numerous denominations, we had to become one in organization. When established, we would elect the officers to govern the affairs of the congregation. The pastor does not govern, but ministers to his flock.

In a quick response from Dr. Boyd, he forwarded a considerable number of directives concerning preparation for organizing an official Methodist congregation. We had to choose all the people who would fill the required offices, all of whom would be elected on the day of organization, which Dr. Boyd had set as May 24, 1964. We had only three weeks to get ready. Our people had chosen the name by which they wanted to be known: the Green Valley Methodist Church.

With great anticipation, we arrived at May 24, 1964, Organization Sunday. Dr. Boyd delivered the morning message and then went through the procedures that brought our group into the fold of Methodism. I had so much appreciation for those with different denominational backgrounds and those who had no church affiliation, who united with their whole hearts in this venture that culminated today. In his closing remarks, Dr. Boyd said he was a little bit jealous of me, in that with more than forty years in ministry he had never been the founding pastor of a new congregation. Needless to say, his remarks made it all worthwhile. I shall never forget this day, this high point in my journey, and all that Jean had done to make it possible.

Talk about finding a building site and plans for a church building filled the air. I was enthused about all this talk, but I knew it would take years for our dream to come true. Time was on our side, as long as we did not wear out our welcome here in the fire hall. It was amazing how reverent everyone felt toward this building.

Having so many irons in the fire since coming to Green Valley, I had, at times, been overwhelmed with fatigue, but now I breathed a little easier, for I had completed my studies for ordination. By God's grace and Jean's help, I had reached another milestone here in June of 1965. Our daughter, Carol, had also reached a milestone in her young life, as she had just graduated from high school. Beginning in September, she would be attending Mount Union College in Alliance, Ohio, which was about ninety-five miles away. Mount Union was a Methodist college, which gave me a clergy discount on tuition. Every little bit helped.

On this day, June 13, 1965, at the age of thirty-nine, I was here at Grove City College in Grove City, Pennsylvania, where all qualified candidates would be ordained. As a candidate, I had chosen two

We were scheduled to have Bishop Roy C. Nichols with us on Sunday, December 8, 1968, to consecrate our building. He would deliver the morning message and then conduct the consecration service. All were excited to have him come and were anxious to show off our new facility, the fruit of much planning and work.

How do you treat a bishop? I wanted everything to go well, but I was a bit nervous. Of course, I would share the service with Bishop Nichols, but what about after the service? The ladies were planning to have refreshments in the fellowship hall for all present. Jean and I talked about having him and Mrs. Nichols come to our home after church for a sit-down dinner with our family and my parents. Through his office we extended our invitation and received a positive reply. In the meantime, my mother agreed to come to our home immediately after church while everyone else was "refreshing" in the fellowship hall. She would finish preparing a meal set up by Jean before we got back from the fellowship hour.

Today was consecration sunday at Green Valley, so we were now official in every aspect. All went well with Bishop Nichols delivering an inspiring message and mixing well with our church family in the fellowship hall. Mom and Dad left immediately after church and came here to our home. They had our meal almost ready by the time we got there. We were blessed by all she did, even doing the table grace. The bishop and Carol hit it off well, as he was on the board at Mount Union College, where she was a student. He was happy to cross-examine a student. Jean rode home with Mrs. Nichols to show her the way, and I drove home with the bishop. We all got better acquainted with each other in the eleven-mile drive. Bishop Nichols was the first African American to hold this office.

As we approached the New Year's holiday, I got a call from Jean at the home of a parishioner I was visiting. She told me Mrs. Boone had called and in a distraught voice shouted that her two sons-in-law had been in a truck accident and that one had been killed and the other was in the hospital. These two young men had just recently purchased a used tractor trailer (an eighteen-wheeler) and started their own business. Mrs. Boone hung up without saying which man had been killed. I was not far away, so I rushed over to her home. She told me David Comara had been killed and that Terry Dunlevy was in critical condition. I had just married David and Debbie last year in October, and on September 13 of this year they had had a baby, David Evan. Terry, who was also a member of our church, had multiple broken bones but was expected to recover. I was told the brakes on their truck had failed on a mountain road in central Pennsylvania and that they had crashed into a deep ravine at a high speed. Today, January 2, 1969, I conducted David's funeral. He was twenty-three. How sad, he and Debbie had just been getting started. This was extremely hard on families, but it was taking a toll on me, as I was so close to those in my congregation. As we moved through this new year, there were other deaths, such as Earl McDaniel, forty-six, our youth coordinator. Each left its mark on all of us.

Today was my forty-fourth birthday, October 19, 1969. The day began well with our usual Sunday school and church services and our drive back home. After lunch, we decided to go for a ride in the country, with Bob riding copilot in the front seat and Jean in the rear with our dog, Heidi. About a block from home, we picked up Frank Cinefra, Bob's friend, who was on his way to visit Bob. Frank sat by the window, with Bob moving to the center. We were enjoying our ride in the country as we entered an intersection just before a speeding car from the right got there. The crash was tremendous. We were hit broadside just forward of the front door, with our car driven into a bank on the opposite side of the intersection. Jean was thrown to the floor, her left knee striking an anchor bolt holding the front seat belt. A large gap opened up over her kneecap. Frank and Bob climbed out through the missing window and all the broken glass. My seat belt was in place, but it had stretched at impact, throwing me against the steering wheel, which had bent badly under my weight.

My knees had each hit the plastic trim strip on each side of the steering post on the dashboard, breaking a hole where each knee hit. Frank and Bob were uninjured and helped Jean and me out of the car. We were both taken to the hospital, treated, and released. Jean was on crutches and I was limping badly with two very sore knees and an aching chest. How blessed we were to survive such a crash and to have no broken bones. What a birthday!

At the moment, information was sketchy, but there should have been a stop sign for us. However, a contractor laying pipe at the intersection had removed it and the stop-sign warning. Both signs were lying in a field near the crash site. The other driver survived, but was taken to the hospital. A most frightening aspect of this crash scene was his mother coming upon the site before he regained consciousness. She thought he was dead.

Amazing things continued to happen on this journey of mine. Remember how we got our first car back in 1948? It was a 1930 Ford Model A. It had been sold to us by Dave Logan at four dollars per week. Well, before the ambulance came, Dave Logan came on the scene. I had never known where he lived, but now I knew. He lived near the intersection, and when he heard the crash, he came running. He asked if he could help in any way. I said it would help if he could take pictures of the accident scene and those signs lying in the field. He replied that he would do that right away. Bob called my dad to come get him and Frank and to make arrangements for a tow truck. The car was severely damaged. I hoped they would total it.

Jean used her crutches for several weeks, and I was rather hobbled for six weeks before getting back to work at the phone company. I was blessed to have good benefits, which paid my wages during my period of recuperation. At church, I missed preaching a couple of Sundays; I had so much pain in my knees, it was hard to stand up for long.

This was a big year for our daughter, Carol. First, she became engaged in April to Garry Lynn Johnson. They had met on a blind date, which was not too unusual, but these two lovebirds had graduated in the same class from high school. The problem was there were around a thousand students in that class, and it was nearly impossible to know everybody. Carol then graduated on June 15, 1969, from Mount Union College with a major in history. Teaching jobs in history were not available in our region, so she went to work for AT&T in the Pittsburgh sales office. Her fiancé, Lynn, was in the US Army and was likely to end up with a tour of duty in Vietnam. Well, yesterday, the day after Christmas, I had the privilege of uniting them in marriage here in the Green Valley Methodist Church, which made it a big year for Dad also. It was a cold and snowy day, and everyone was happy that the wedding reception was there in the fellowship hall. The women of the church decorated and prepared everything. It was just wonderful and so appreciated.

A New Decade

We were in the middle of January 1970, and we had just got our car back from our accident. The insurance company had refused to write it off. I cannot describe all the damage, but all four fenders were damaged. Both bumpers had to be replaced and the whole car had to be repainted, along with other damage to the engine. I did not feel safe in this vehicle. My friend, Dave Logan, took pictures of the accident scene and the missing signs lying in the field near the intersection. We hired an attorney and gave him the pictures.

Throughout all these weeks of repairing our wrecked car, we had the use of my sister, Audrey, and Dick, my brother-in-law's, second car, a Ford Falcon. This was three months of inconvenience for them, but a blessing to us. I kept giving them a progress report on car repairs, feeling guilty as weeks grew into months, but they told me not to be so apologetic. We were truly grateful for their help. There was no excuse for a Chrysler dealership to take so long to repair our car.

Jean and I were not comfortable with our rebuilt car, so we traded it for an American Motors Ambassador. The other car was a beauty, a 1968 two-door hardtop with a black vinyl roof and a silver body. The Ambassador was a four-door car and was two-tone green.

Today, February 8, following the benediction, I addressed the congregation about the snow in the church parking lot. I urged them to make sure everyone got onto the street. Everybody got out without any trouble, except for one family in a two-tone green Ambassador, who needed several men to rescue them.

I have not mentioned this before, but in my neck I have several degenerative discs, which give me unbearable headaches when I am under stress or if I tilt my head back too far in looking upward. I had been hospitalized with this condition and at times I wore a neck collar. Stress comes in all shapes and sizes, nowhere more than in the ministry. When my people hurt, I hurt, and when I hurt, the stress takes over. I was so close to my people. We had grown together in these nearly seven years, and the years had been mostly joyful. I had been so blessed in my ministry in Green Valley. By the way, this church, which had "valley" in its name, sat on the highest level in this working-class community.

With Palm Sunday behind us and Easter 1970 just days away, this should be such a glorious time, but sad news clouded this Holy Week. Jimmy Collura and his friends had been playing cowboys and Indians in a field not far from our church building. In his attempt to hide, he had crouched down behind a huge boulder and sat down, leaning against the boulder. Shortly, that boulder moved toward him, pinning him in a way that made it impossible for him to breathe. Jimmy died on the spot. It took ten men to move that boulder, which had been there for several years. Jimmy was nine years old. I recalled how he had dashed over the cushions of our communion kneeler during our last communion service in the fire hall. Sadly, I would have his funeral the day before Easter.

I had prayed over what I should do about my situation as pastor to the Green Valley congregation. I loved these people, but I was convinced that they should have a full-time pastor, not someone like me, who worked forty hours per week at the telephone company. I offer this comment not as an apology, for under the circumstances, I believe I served my people well. Throughout my ministry in Green Valley, I averaged one pastoral call per day, which would indicate what I had been doing on my days off at the phone company. I was at the point of burnout, which was not good for me, my family, the phone company, or these people I had come to love. Therefore, I met with our district superintendent, William Daugherty, the man who baptized our children and conducted the funeral for the child we lost. He agreed with my assessment and would bring in a full-time pastor on the first Sunday in July 1970.

When this news greeted the congregation, it was not well received. I believe mostly that over the years we had become so close in love and work that a change was not a high priority, nor something that was thought about. However, in these weeks since the news broke, all was calm and the congregation held a farewell dinner for Jean and me and gave us a gift of luggage and a nice attaché case. The hardest part about this sendoff was it took place before my last sermon on June 28, which was like saying goodbye twice. At last count, our membership was 267, a great leap from my first Sunday in September 1963.

Prior to my last day in the pulpit, I met with the incoming pastor to acquaint him with his new assignment. I had a sense that he was not enthused over coming to the Green Valley church. I offered whatever help I could along with emphasis on how much Curwen Colflesh had helped me in the communion services and how much it meant to Curwen to be a part of it. The new pastor held his first communion service the first Sunday in October, Worldwide Communion Sunday. I do not know whether he ever approached Curwen, but on that Sunday morning Curwen did not come to church. Curwen had committed suicide at home that morning. Only God knows why, but I have my thoughts about the why of it. I lost a dear friend.

With the knowledge that my tenure at Green Valley was ending on June 28, I assured myself that I would take a year off before taking another church. Without my knowing, my name and phone number were given to the district superintendent of the Pittsburgh area. He wanted to meet me at the Mount Washington United Methodist Church, high on the mount above the city. I met with him and some members of that congregation. He explained they had lost their pastor on the Sunday I left Green Valley and asked me to take over. I was well armed with excuses for saying no, but I said yes. I did not even get one Sunday off. However, my "teammate," Jean, and I entered this venture with enthusiasm, her teaching Sunday school and me preaching. The only way I could fill this obligation was to rehash some of my old sermons in weeks where I just did not have the wherewithal to produce something new. I could not get over how many of my old sermons were not worth rehashing. After all, I had thought they were good when I first delivered them. They were filling my round file.

With our first year at Mount Washington behind us, Jean and I were quite happy with our situation. Right now, Jean was in the Magee Women's Hospital with some female problems, and I was lying in traction in Saint Francis Hospital with a major problem with those degenerative discs in my neck. We had each been hospitalized one week. I got to visit Jean once before I became a patient here. Bob was home alone, wondering how to handle his parents in separate hospitals. And Carol and Lynn, upon his return from Vietnam, had moved to Washington, DC, where he was now stationed at Fort McNair.

Jean was released after two weeks and had Alverta Reid, a member of the Green Valley church and a nurse, caring for her. I was out after nineteen days in traction. While I was hospitalized, two management people from the phone company had visited me. They were aware that some of the work I did in adjusting relays, and welding contacts on some, was aggravating my neck condition. They told me to think about some other job in the company I would like to have and that they would try to get it for me. Wow! I was stunned by their offer. Should I start at the top? Seriously, I did not have anything in mind. I liked what I had been doing.

Several weeks after returning to work, I was approached about a job in downtown Pittsburgh. It would be a desk job answering trouble calls and dispatching troubleshooters for repairs. The pay grade would be the same; however, the work hours would be from five in the evening to one in the morning. There would be added to my pay a 10 percent differential. If I were to take this job, it would add years to my time with the phone company, as this neck problem was surely going to put me out on disability. I chose to take this job and had to adjust to it and the strange hours. Jean was having a harder time, being alone in the evenings, but at least we were together during the day. Of course, on some days, I visited the people in my congregation. I started this new job in October 1971.

One major problem caused by the new job was that Jean was not only home alone, but she was without a car. Jean and I stopped in at our American Motors dealership today and bought a brand-new Gremlin, which was a small two-door car with a stick shift. My bride had no trouble with a stick shift. She took Bob out after school teaching him how to drive a stick shift.

In these writings, I have alluded to some of my experiences in building things, such as having made the kitchen cabinets for our home while the building was under construction. I have always liked doing woodworking projects and working with concrete. Since moving into this home, I had added a porch and built an eight-by-eight-foot concrete-block tool shed. With my back injury from World War II and the degenerative discs in my neck, I suffered pain and discomfort, but I was too stubborn to lie around making excuses for being unable to do something.

What I am leading up to is this: I had designed a twenty-four-by-twenty-five-foot garage to house our travel trailer and our new Gremlin. Now, I wanted to build this garage. First, it would take a concrete footer, two courses of concrete block, and then a poured concrete slab twenty-four by twenty-five feet. Then ten-foot walls, a nine-by-sixteen-foot double door, and a thirty-six-inch entrance door, topped off with prefabbed trusses for the roof. It meant laying one thousand concrete blocks, requiring considerable scaffolding in the process. My back ached just thinking about this project, but I was going to build this garage.

My ministry at Mount Washington was going well, and Jean and I felt comfortable with everyone. One man stood out. His name was Russ Loomis. He was the lay leader of this congregation, and he taught the adult Bible class. I enjoyed being in his class and conversing with him about the affairs of this congregation. He was at the top in knowledge about what was going on. Russ preached when I was away. He had taken care of everything while I was hospitalized. When I assumed the pastor's duties here, the superintendent had told me I would close this church, as attendance was so poor. Attendance was in the forty-five to fifty range when I came here, and with some visitation it increased to the midsixties. In a sanctuary that could hold four hundred people, it looked empty with sixty-five spread out over the pews. Jean had been well received and loved teaching Sunday school and working with me in the youth fellowship group.

With my new job at the phone company, I had far fewer severe headaches such as I had in my previous location. In fact, I had not missed a day of work since I had changed jobs. Now that was a period of only seven months, but it was a record for me.

As we approached the spring of 1972, I had shown my garage plans to the code-enforcement people and been granted a building permit. So far I had installed the footer with two courses of block. Our son, Bob, and his friend Randy Leroy had been working to level the surface in preparation for pouring the concrete slab. Together, we put in all the reinforcing wire for the floor. My friend John Mitchell, a contractor, volunteered to have the concrete blocks delivered to my building site, while having their cost billed to his account. Thus, I received a contractor's discount, a considerable savings on a thousand blocks.

The concrete was delivered and I had much help on hand. Before Bob and Randy leveled the ground, I had put in sewers and waterlines underground. In the exact center of the floor, there was a floor drain embedded in a four-by-four-foot concrete square. This gave me an island from which to hold one end of the board for leveling the concrete from the center to the slab edges. My Dad, Bob, and some neighbors helped spread the concrete. As the leveled mass was setting up, my neighbor Phil Giuffre and I began troweling the surface. This was a tough exercise in the best of circumstances, but today the sun was so hot that the concrete was drying too rapidly. We had to keep spraying a mist of water ahead of our work. Except for the last few feet, we ended up with a pretty good finish overall.

Having allowed curing time for the garage floor, I began to lay the concrete blocks. This was not my profession, so I thought it best to go slowly. Early on I learned that I could lay twenty-two blocks from one sack of premixed mortar. That became my standard, lay twenty-two blocks each morning and then clean up and go to work at the phone company. This was going to be a long process, but the best way to guard my health.

Within three weeks, I had laid enough blocks to have a wall four feet high along the sides and rear of my garage. Jean, Bob, and I decided to take a long vacation, so we hooked up the travel trailer and headed for Canada. We entered Canada through the state of Minnesota and headed west with the goal of reaching Vancouver Island on the Pacific Coast. We enjoyed the wonderful scenery along the way and made a second visit in the town of Banff, where we had stayed several years ago. We did our best to revisit all the national parks in this beautiful country. Reaching the West Coast, we put the car and trailer on a ferry out to Vancouver Island. The high point of our time on the island was a visit to Butchart Gardens, a vast and flowering area that had transformed a stone quarry into something spectacular in its beauty.

After a wonderful Canadian vacation, we took the ferry to the state of Washington. We entered at Port Angeles and headed south along the coast. We parked the trailer on the beach for the night and had such a delightful time. The next day, we went over to Mount Rainer and drove up as high as the road would allow. There was much snow up there, higher than the car. When we looked at our maps, we realized how far we were from home and that we better head east. We had a great vacation and saw a lot of beautiful sights, but there is no place like home.

Having been away for three weeks, there was a lot of catching up to do. I had to check up on my congregation through Russ Loomis, who had handled things in my absence. My block laying would have to wait a few days while I attended to more pressing matters. Over the years, Jean and I had been blessed in our travels to visit forty-eight states on the mainland, as well as much of Canada. It was great to have Bob with us on our latest trip sharing the driving with me. It is a little tougher towing a trailer. He graduated from high school this year and would be off to college in the fall.

All was well at the Mount Washington church, and I was back to my preaching duties and visitations. At the phone company, I was back on my 5:00 p.m. to 1:00 a.m. schedule. I had been making good progress in laying blocks on my garage. On some of my days off, I laid forty-four blocks instead of twenty-two. I was nearing the ten-foot height on the walls.

One of my supervisors at the phone company, Fran Dixon, did electrical work. He followed my progress in constructing the garage and told me he would wire my building for cost of materials only. He told me to cut holes in the walls where I wanted electrical outlets and to fish the walls, leaving a length of heavy cord in place for him to pull in the wires. This was a generous offer, and I complied with his instructions as I reached the ten-foot height all around the building. I put a wood cap on top of the blocks, and Bob and I put up all the trusses for the roof and covered them with four-by-eight-foot plywood sheets. We covered the plywood with tar paper.

Fran came here and wired the garage, including the installation of a fuse box. I assisted the best I could. I was so thankful for Fran's generosity. Now that I was ready to shingle the roof, my coworker Larry Leubert volunteered to give me a day of his time and talent to help me do this job. I was so blessed to have all this help. Bob kept us busy supplying the shingles. Larry and I did not quite finish the roof, so I was able to complete the job on my own, about a four-hour job.

With the building under roof and wired professionally, I had to price out the materials for a nine-by-sixteen-foot garage door. Just as I was about to buy the door and hardware, a contractor stopped and asked if he could give me a bid on the full job, with him supplying all parts and labor. I said yes. When he gave me the bid, it was almost exactly what I was going to pay for the materials.

Wow, what a break! The contractor was Bill Jansen. He had been a year behind me in high school.

With the door installed, Phil Giuffre volunteered to drywall the ceiling with sheeting left over from jobs he had worked. Phil was a drywall expert. One evening, while I worked my five-to-one shift, Phil and his son, Dan, came over and finished the ceiling, with no cost to me. Think about this: in many places in these writings, I have acknowledged my belief in a Silent Partner watching over me and directing timely blessings toward me. Did He have anything to do with all the volunteers who came forward to help completing my garage? My answer is yes! Remember those who helped lay the concrete floor, the contractor who got me a discount on the blocks, the friend who did the wiring, the coworker who gave a day of his time to install shingles, the contractor friend who showed up at just the right moment to bid on my garage door, and the neighbor who put in the ceiling at no cost? I did not seek any of this aid, yet it came in timely, godlike blessings. My Silent Partner never rests. I am truly grateful for all who were a part of this project, and I hope you enjoy the picture of the finished garage.

Bob, our son, now attended a community college about six miles away, so he was living at home. He was using our little "Gremlin" for transportation, and would be back home in time for Jean to have the car should she need it.

Here, in the spring of 1973, I was happy to report that I had perfect attendance at my job at the phone company, a real accomplishment for me, and it was met with great approval by my employer. However, on the church front, I had quite a scare as I was removing my clergy robe after the April 22 morning worship service. A strange, indescribable feeling came over me and a sense that I was having a stroke. I was alone in the changing room and sat down. After several minutes, all seemed normal and I met Jean as she waited for me, wondering why I was late. I told her what had happened and that I would be going to see a doctor in the morning. The doctor could not pinpoint a problem, but came down hard on me about my schedule in working two jobs. He insisted I give up one of those jobs.

I could not ask for the doctor's advice and then ignore it. My first reaction was to not preach the following Sunday, but have Russ Loomis fill the pulpit. I told Russ I was going to tell the district superintendent to assign another pastor to the Mount Washington church, as I was resigning at the end of June. It was a sad ending to a pastorate that I had enjoyed very much. My congregation fully understood the threat to my health. Jean and I were overwhelmed by their love and good wishes. Russ really touched my heart when he told me I had been one of the three most influential people in his life. What a most rewarding compliment. I was humbled by this. I had been officially succeeded by another pastor. I was now at ease and had returned to the Rosedale church where I first entered the ministry. Right now I enjoying being preached to instead of preaching. Amen!

I was relaxed and feeling good. Jean and I purchased golf clubs and had been going out to a nine-hole golf course, just having fun trying to get the hang of this game. Scores did not matter. What mattered was that Jean and I could be out together having a good time. This golf course was owned by Bob and Kass McMahon, and we often played the course with them. Occasionally they had someone else, usually Bob's sister, run the course while the four of us traveled some distance for lunch.

On this journey, I related the details of the kidney-stone attack I had in 1951 in Illinois, requiring hospitalization while on vacation. Well, over these past twenty-two years, I had been hospitalized two more times and had passed more than forty kidney stones. In the past year, I had decided to give up drinking iced tea, which I always drank instead of water. I did this on my own, and praise God, I had not had another attack.

I mentioned having returned to the Rosedale church following the end of my pastoring at the Mount Washington church. It was difficult adjusting to not preaching each Sunday. I was ill at ease, and yet I did not have an overwhelming desire to have my own church. Somehow, I thought going back to the church of my youth would be helpful. I convinced Jean to make such a move. We transferred to Verona Methodist Church, whose pastor was Ray Jones. He had been ordained in the same class as myself. This was a rewarding move for me, as I became reacquainted with people I had known since childhood. Jean was patiently getting to know a lot of new people and was adjusting well. Back in the church of my childhood, I was asked to preach a few times in the absence of the pastor, and I enjoyed these opportunities.

This year, 1974, passed rapidly, but something that did not pass rapidly was the settlement from that auto accident we had in October of 1969. We had just received a settlement, minus attorney's fees. It was not large, but it was welcome. Also, this year brought us the first resignation in our history of a president of the United States of America, Richard M. Nixon. Gerald R. Ford ascended to the presidency without ever having run for office, nor had he sought his previous office as vice president. This was a stunning happening in our nation's history. This gives opportunity for some name dropping. On our first trip to California in 1964, we visited my cousin, Bonnie Bell Wardman, who lived on Summit Drive in Whittier. She showed us a huge dining room in which she and her husband, Aubrey, a Southern California oil and telephone magnate, had entertained Vice President Nixon when he was in town to speak at Whittier College. Upon her death, her beautiful home was willed to Whittier College. It was my hope that President Ford would be capable of handling this job that has been placed on his shoulders.

These past couple of years had been so good. For one thing, I had had perfect attendance on my job at the phone company since 1971. Jean and I continued taking extensive vacations and played a lot of golf. For the present, we played only at Bob and Kass's nine-hole course and were both getting better at this game. At the Verona church, they voted me to be their assistant pastor and, by agreement, an unpaid assistant.

Between Christmas and New Year's 1976, Mom Simpson was involved in a serious automobile accident when a car pulled out of a filling station, into her path, and she hit it broadside. The other driver's grandmother was killed instantly. Mom suffered numerous injuries, the most serious being a concussion as a result of her head smashing against the windshield. She was hospitalized for a while and then returned to her apartment. In mid-March, she suffered a stroke and died a few days later on March 22. Jean and I were in Illinois and had just gotten back to sister Jane's home after a visit with Mom when we received word from the hospital informing us that she had just passed away. We stayed on after the funeral to clear Mom's apartment of her belongings. Jim and Jane handled the legal affairs, which were so time consuming.

It seemed like there was going to be something new in our lives. We got a letter from Lee White, my former shipmate, announcing that he had scheduled a ship's crew reunion this year over Independence Day weekend 1976. Our first reunion had been in 1950, which I mentioned earlier. At that time, a collection had been taken and given to a shipmate who was supposed schedule another reunion. In twenty-six years, he had done nothing. Well, we would be meeting in Syracuse, New York, thanks to Lee.

With all things settled over Mom's passing, we made our reunion plans. It had been sad for both of us, but especially for Jean, as only her twin sister was left of her immediate family. The distance to Syracuse was 370 miles. I was looking forward to seeing the "men of war," whom I had not seen since leaving *LST-1024* in January 1946.

We arrived at the motel, the site of our reunion, and met quite a crowd of shipmates and their wives. Some of my mates were readily recognizable, and others looked like total strangers, but it was such a glorious get-together, somewhat of a tearjerker. We were all so thankful for what Lee had done to bring thirty-two men into this wonderful relationship after all these years. After three days together, we voted to have another reunion in two years, perhaps in St. Louis.

It seemed like President Ford had just got into office and now had been turned away as a result of this November's election. He would be succeeded by Jimmy Carter on January 20, 1977. I sat down and wrote the following letter to President Ford.

Dear President Ford,

I want to thank you for what you've done for our country. I don't believe any man has ever assumed the Office of the President of the United States of America under more challenging circumstances than you did with the resignation of Richard M. Nixon. It is not my purpose to relate all the pitfalls in your path when the burden of the Presidency was placed upon your shoulders, but to praise and thank you for the forthright way in which you went about bringing trust and respect to that great office. No man is ever truly prepared for the weight of the office, even when he seeks it, but you rose to the occasion in a manner deserving of the eternal gratitude of all Americans. This may sound like a hollow statement on the heels of Mr. Carter's victory on November 2nd, but your "good works" will be appropriately recorded in history. "Well done, Thou good and faithful servant."

It saddens me that you will not continue to be our nation's leader, but time will heal that wound. As for your immediate future . . . take time to be yourself, to be to your lovely wife, Betty, and family, all the things the demands of public service have kept you from being except for a few fleeting moments over the years. Thank you, Mr. President, and may God richly bless you and yours.

Most sincerely,
Charles F. Remaley, Jr.

I wrote that letter to President Ford on November 11 and received a response on November 30. Here is his response:

November 30, 1976

Dear Mr. Remaley:

Your kind message is deeply appreciated.

Long after the hard work and hurried pace of the campaign are forgotten, I will remember the generous encouragement and goodwill which were extended to me and my entire family by our fellow Americans. It has been a tremendous honor to serve the people of our great country, and I will never forget this wonderful privilege.

Mrs. Ford and I thank you from our hearts for your friendship, and send you our warmest good wishes for the future.

Sincerely,
Gerald R. Ford

Carol, our daughter, worked for AT&T in Pittsburgh for a brief time, and then transferred to another AT&T office in Washington, DC, when her husband, Lynn, returned from Vietnam. After Lynn's discharge from the US Army, he worked in the tire business for several years, but eventually he too became an employee of AT&T in Washington, DC. Jean and I visited them frequently in their new home. One day they took us on a tour of DC, which included a trip to the Smithsonian Institute. As we walked through a display section on communications, we came upon a piece of telephone equipment I had worked on many years ago in the Montrose Central Office in Pittsburgh. When I first worked on it after finishing switchman's school, I mentioned that it was not the kind of equipment I had studied in that course and that it had been so obsolete it should be in a museum. Well, it had done just that. It was such a thrill to have been there to see something I had helped maintain during my career.

Having used travel trailers for the past twelve years, Jean and I decided to buy a small motor home, a self-contained unit, with all the necessities, such as a shower, toilet, stove, and refrigerator. We had sold our travel trailer to Pastor Jones, who had taken it to a campground. We settled on a Dodge "maxi van" with a raised roof. It lacked cabinet space, so I ordered two sheets of plywood that matched the cabinets supplied by the factory. The plywood was in the motor home when it was delivered. I made and placed more cabinets in every conceivable area of our new motor home.

With everything in order, we packed our motor home with clothes, food, and supplies for a trip to Florida. We anticipated having a great time in the Sunshine State. Of course, we stopped along the way in trailer parks for overnight stays. We always felt safe in these surroundings. Once in Florida, we headed to Disney World and had a wonderful day in the park. Much of it resembled Disneyland in California, which we had visited in 1964. We then crossed the state to the Gulf of Mexico, visiting whatever attractions were available along the way. Near Tampa Bay, we visited my high school classmate, Al Torchia, whom you will recall spent time as a prisoner of war in Germany. After a brief visit, we headed north along the Gulf Coast, working our way back to Pennsylvania.

Jean was anxious to get back home. She missed doing her daily crossword puzzles. I believe she would rather start her day doing a puzzle than with breakfast. She also spent time doing various kinds of needlework, producing beautiful pictures of jungle animals, flowers, birds, butterflies, dogs, kittens, and scenes of early America. When Jean finished a picture, I made a wooden frame for it. She did such beautiful work and would rip out a large portion if she saw an error in a stitch. It had to be perfect, just like she was. I loved her so.

Getting back to work after a great vacation could help me improve on my absentee record. After achieving more than six years of perfect attendance, I had been missing a lot of work with severe headaches caused by the degenerative discs in my neck. So far, nobody had spoken to me about this problem, but if I did not improve, they had justification for warning me. I used neck traction at home and wore a neck collar much of the time. This job was an after-hours trouble-report center where 100 percent of the calls involved trouble with somebody's phone. Most people wanted immediate repairs. Nobody was calling in to tell you what a nice guy you were. At times, this job was quite tense. Hence, headaches. I was blessed to have had these thirty-two years with the phone company. They had been good to me.

Over the years, we had done many things with Jack and Mamie Felger, visiting each other and travelling together on short trips. They were among our closest friends during these past thirty years. We also looked forward to being with them at future Navy reunions. Good friends are so hard to find. This friendship began in World War II.

Through 1979 and 1980, Jean and I had such good times using our motor home, sometimes on trips to places hundreds of miles away. On many occasions, we went to a nearby state park that had a lake and rental canoes. We usually had enough food for two meals, so we would spend the day canoeing and relaxing. We had more time to relax now that I had given up my responsibilities as assistant pastor of Verona Methodist Church.

Into Retirement

I was in the midst of what looked like the end of my career as a telephone employee. In early October 1980, I was called into my supervisor's office about my absenteeism. I offered no defense, as the record was there before me. The headaches had become so bad that on one shift, I just lay down on the floor beside my desk until the shift was over, and then a coworker had driven me home. I had informed my supervisor that I had an appointment the following morning with a neurosurgeon. The next morning, upon examination and review of my history, along with my poor work-attendance record, the surgeon stated I could no longer go back to work. She advised me to not undergo surgery, as the degeneration in my neck discs made it unwise. I immediately called my office informing them of the doctor's report. The company standard was that if I did not improve and pass their physical exam before the passing of one year, I would be put off the work roll and onto a disability pension, which was 50 percent of my base pay. Meanwhile, I was drawing my full base pay. I could not ask for better treatment.

During the past year, leading up to this month, October 1981, the telephone company doctors would not okay me for a return to work. Thus, I was now on a disability pension. I would be fifty-six years old on the nineteenth of this month. Living on half pay would be a tight squeeze, but we had no choice. Our mortgage would not be paid off until 1985, and we had no other debt. On pension, the company covered Jean and me with a very good healthcare plan at no cost to me.

In early 1982, a high-level management person from the telephone company called me and said that, in reviewing my disability case, they felt I was qualified for Social Security disability. They advised me to file a claim. I filed such a claim, but after a couple of months of waiting I was turned down. I was advised to file a second claim, which I did, only to be turned down again. However, in the "turn-down" notice, it was suggested that if I wished to pursue my case, get a lawyer. I heeded that advice and made an appointment with Robert Pierce, a former county commissioner and an attorney in Pittsburgh. Gathering all my medical records and employment status, we went to court, presenting our case before a judge. My case was discussed openly and completely. The judge said he would study my situation and render a decision within a few days. In about a week I was informed that I had been awarded a favorable verdict and that I would be placed on Social Security disability.

The attorney and the phone company worked together to settle everything. It was determined that Social Security would be retroactive to the day I went on disability. This meant a lump sum of money had accumulated on my behalf. Out of this sum I was required to repay the company the difference between what would have been my earned pension and the disability pension they had paid me. The attorney's fees were then deducted, and I received a check covering the balance. Wow! What a heavenly blessing; my Silent Partner was still looking after me. I was so grateful.

In full retirement and with adequate income, Jean and I were able to have so much time together. We still went out and played nine holes of golf. Most of the time I was playing golf I wore my neck collar. It looked rather stupid, but it reminded me not to swing too hard. On one occasion, we were on the tee of a hole when a golfer going toward a green had a wild shot heading in my direction. As I leaped, trying to get out of the way, the ball struck me on the ankle, spinning me around and knocking me to the ground. I was not hurt, but the golfer jumped into his cart and came toward me at high speed. He was in a panic over hitting me, and even more so when he realized I was wearing a neck collar. I assured him no harm was done. He apologized and kept coming my way at each hole to make sure I was okay. I was most thankful that the ball did not hit Jean, the love of my life.

Speaking of golf, on another occasion, as Jean and I were golfing, I dubbed my drive and from where my ball landed, I could not see the green. Jean outdrove me, and in my disgust (not because she outdrove me, but my poor shot), I approached the ball and smacked it with all my might. I hoped it would go toward the green. When we reached the green, my ball was not in sight, and as Jean played onto the green, I approached a large sand trap, expecting to find my ball.

Just as I shouted to Jean that my ball was not in the trap, she, in her sweet voice, addressed me. "Red, there is a ball in the cup. Could it be yours?"

Hey, what is wrong with a little luck? It was a short par-four hole, and I had made it in two for the only eagle I would ever have. It's a wonderful world.

Robert Walker, who had been best man in our wedding, informed me that a dinner honoring President Ford was going to be held in the retirement community where he held a management position. I asked him to get us tickets for the event. On June 12, 1983, Jean and I arrived and were greeted by Bob and his wife, Jean, who had both been in my class in high school. While waiting for dinner, Jean and I were walking around checking out the beauty of this spacious community. We observed President Ford standing alone in an out-of-the-way spot. I suggested to Jean that we approach him. We walked up to him and greeted him as Mr. President, introducing ourselves. After some brief pleasantries, I said, "Mr. President, I have a letter in my pocket from you, which I believe has a stamped signature. Would you honor me by signing it live?" He pleasantly filled my request, and I felt so honored.

Jean and I were so close and so in love. We were unbiased in our heartfelt belief in God and His strong providence in our lives. As you have read in these pages, we lived a life of ups and downs, but mostly ups, for which we were grateful. In the downs, God was always with us, giving us the wherewithal to endure in the hour of challenge. In the love Jean and I had for each other, it was surely the handiwork of God. He connected the dots of two people who had lived five hundred miles apart.

With so much time on my hands and a strong desire to get involved in woodworking, I walled off a portion of my garage, creating space for a woodshop. Then I purchased most all the power tools I would need for craftwork. One of my earliest projects was making a grandmother's clock for Jean from a kit. It turned out beautifully and played chimes throughout the day. I made footstools and clocks. I designed the wooden clocks' exteriors and placed quartz timepiece units within those clock casings. I gave a lot of them away and sold some at craft shows. Some were wall clocks, others were small desk clocks or mantle clocks.

My parents always told me, as a child, that the older you become, the faster the time flies. I now understood that fully. Here we were on September 14, 1986, celebrating forty years of wedded bliss. While Jean and I thought forty years were a lot, my parents would be celebrating sixty-four years of marriage on the twenty-fifth. They were both eighty-three years old.

Through my Christian upbringing and in my studies, I continually came across the adage that what people see in you is a sermon in their minds. We go through this life not knowing whether our life has shed light on the path of another. On rare occasions, we learn that we had a positive influence where we never imagined. The reason I bring this up is that I received a letter from a former neighbor who was a career Army officer, a major. His outfit was stationed at the Pittsburgh International Airport. In his letter, he thanked me for bringing him into a closer walk with Christ. I cannot put into words how much this letter meant to me. The lesson: if someone has had a positive influence on us, thank them. It will make a difference to them. The bookmark in my Bible has this quote: "What you are is God's gift to you. What you make of yourself is your gift to God." And I add, "And to others!"

This journey of mine has been so full of many wonderful things. As we moved into the 1990s, I was especially grateful for all the

Navy reunions Lee White produced and for the endless hours and miles he travelled to find the men of our crew. We had had great times together, and we rejoiced when someone new showed up. At one reunion—remember Mr. Nichols?—he showed up. At the hotel, there was a balcony high above the check-in desk. Someone pointed down to the desk and said, "That is Nichols signing in." His first name was Anthony, but I had never called him anything but Mr. Nichols as an officer. He was no longer my officer, so I wondered what to call him. I had not seen him in thirty years. I shouted toward the desk, "Hi Tony!" Without even looking up he shouted, "Hi Red!" I must have made quite an impression on this man who recognized my voice after thirty years. We shook hands and had a tension-free time together, unlike our time aboard ship.

Here on October 27, 1990, Bob and his fiancée were married. Her name was Debbie and we loved her so much. She brought joy into our home every time she visited. They had known each other since kindergarten, and we prayed God would bless them richly. Last night we all gathered at the River's Edge restaurant for a wonderful dinner for the bridal party. They would be living in Bob's apartment in Oakmont.

A block away from our home, where our street intersected with Quincy Drive, there was a strip of land that was too small for any legal building. It had always been an eyesore, so little by little I cleared the land and ran my lawn mower over the weeds. This plot of land was about 20 feet by 150 feet. With proceeds from my craft products, we purchased and installed a two-rail fence along the edge of this land where it dropped away precipitously—a danger to children. I attached some wire fencing to the rails to discourage pass-through. As funds and time permitted, I would put in a lawn and flower beds. After installing the rail fence, with Jean's help, we went on vacation. When we returned home, we discovered that sixteen of those rails had been broken. Neighbors said that a drunk man had done the damage, but nobody could identify him. It was harder to replace those rails than it had been to build the fence in the first place.

Life was moving so rapidly that I had trouble keeping up with the times. I have mentioned how we had bonded with Jack and Mamie Felger, doing things together, visiting each other. This past Friday, they came over from Ohio, and we spent the day travelling here in western Pennsylvania, had lunch, and then returned home. Before they headed for Ohio, I took them to see my parents. My mother had just gotten home from the doctor's office.

She said, "I feel like a pincushion. The doctor gave me a flu shot in one arm and a pneumonia shot in the other."

I thought this was strange, as at the age of ninety she had never had either of these shots. After our visit, Mom and Dad saw us to the door, and as we were leaving, I reminded them that I would be picking them up the next morning to take them to a church luncheon. Nine hours later, at 2:10 a.m., Dad phoned me and told me to come quickly. Mom was having trouble breathing. Upon arrival, I called 911. They responded immediately, but she had passed away, four days before her ninety-first birthday and just a few days after her and Dad's seventy-second wedding anniversary. Her passing was on October 8, 1994.

Looking back on Mom's passing and the celebration of my parents' seventy-two years of marriage, I am in awe over such an accomplishment and the wealth of good health during all those years. Here, on September 14, 1996, Bob and Carol honored Jean and me with a fantastic "Golden Wedding" anniversary party held in Oakmont's Chelsea Grille. They invited so many of our friends and relatives from out of state, as well as local. This was not a surprise event, so I received a call from my dear friend Jimmy Maddy, expressing his and Agnes's regrets, but they did send us a gift. Then, as the affair began, they walked in laughing about how they had pulled one over on us by coming in from New Mexico. It was a joy to see them. Tom and Barbara Fritz came from Virginia— remember, these two men helped move us into our home forty-one years ago. I do not know how many were there. We were honored by their presence, especially my best man, Bob Walker, and his wife, Jean, who came in from South Carolina. Also, two of our bridesmaids were there: Jane, Jean's twin, and Audrey, my sister. We had the grandest time and were so indebted to Carol and Bob for this unforgettable affair.

That golden wedding party had been so uplifting to Jean and me. To be so loved by our children and so honored by so many friends and relatives could not help but energize us for the years ahead, however many that may be. We had added years in age and to our marital years, but continued playing golf and visited our favorite restaurants two or three times a week. In my old age, at seventy-five, I received a call from Reverend Paul Millikan, pastor of the Trinity Tower United Methodist Church here in our community. He wanted to know if I would be interested in being the visiting pastor for his congregation. I told him I would take the job, but not take any wages. I agreed to accept reimbursements for gasoline. I was happy to do this, and I was meeting so many wonderful people.

Everything was going along so well, but all, at the moment, was shattered by the terrorist attacks here on September 11, 2001. In the midst of the attacks, word was out that President George W. Bush had been in a schoolroom in Florida when his chief of staff, Andy Card, alerted him about what was happening. We learned that he, in Air Force One, had taken off from Florida, and there was fear that plane would be shot down. This news struck home with us because we knew that Eddie Marinzel, our niece Sue's husband, was on that plane with the president. Eddie, at the moment, was head of the White House Secret Service. Of course, the plane's whereabouts were top secret. In talking to Eddie, I learned that he and Andy Card had to overrule the president in his desire to get back to Washington, DC, immediately. Once the air space was clear and safe for the president, they returned to Washington.

The days following the 9/11 attack were filled with unending news reports covering the incident and the implications of it all. It was a steady drumbeat, not unwarranted, but overwhelming in volume. During these days of news highlights and growing tensions over what would follow, my dad, age ninety-eight, kept himself glued to all news reports and became very upset about it all. Dad lived alone, but was only three blocks away from us. A few days after the attack, on September 16, Dad called here and told Jean to come quickly, he was dying. We rushed to his home and found him extremely weak but rational. I called 911 and in just a few minutes, an ambulance was on scene. In less than an hour at the hospital, we were informed that Dad was bleeding internally and they were giving him a blood transfusion. We left the hospital late that night once they had him stabilized, as he seemed to be in good spirits. At 9:30 the next morning, the report from the hospital was that Dad was doing well and they were still giving him blood. I arrived at the hospital at 10:30 a.m. and was met in the hallway by a doctor. He informed me that, in the middle of a conversation, Dad passed away. There was no autopsy, but it is my belief that Dad may have had an aneurysm on the aorta, which both my sister and I had, which may have burst. His death was so sudden. I loved him and I miss him.

For many years, we have had Remaley family reunions in Meadville, Pennsylvania. This was our first reunion without Dad since his passing last year. This year, just after our meal, Jean got up from the table and stepped backward far enough for her right foot to drop off the edge of the pavilion's concrete floor. Her foot jammed between the concrete and a large ice chest. Losing her balance, she fell over backward, twisting her leg and breaking it in three places. The breaks were near her knee and so severe that a knee replacement could not be done. They repaired the damage using a couple of steel plates. Jean was hospitalized for a few days and then sent to a rehabilitation center. Our daughter, Carol, witnessed some strange remarks made by Jean following the surgery. Upon Jean's return home, she had zero interest in doing a crossword puzzle, which was one of her great loves. I shared my concern with her doctor, and in early 2003 she was diagnosed as suffering from dementia. Prior to the operation, there had not been a trace of dementia. Jean recovered wonderfully from the leg injury and was walking well. However, her golfing days were over.

Al Webeck, a member of the Trinity Tower United Methodist Church, where I was now the visiting pastor, invited me to play golf with him. We had played weekly for a while, but he went south to Myrtle Beach, South Carolina, each fall. In the course of conversations with Al, I learned that he attended a Methodist church during the winter, where the pastor's name was Charlie. One Sunday evening I was talking on the phone with my best man, Bob Walker, who lived in Myrtle Beach and attended a Methodist church. I asked Bob if his pastor's name was Charlie. He said yes. Then I told him my golfing buddy went to the same church during the winter. When I gave him Al's name, he said, "I talked to him in church this morning." Further, Bob told me they had played golf together. Is this a small world, or what? Sadly, my friend Al had some health issues, was hospitalized in Myrtle Beach, and died.

After three years as a visiting pastor, I decided to retire full time. There were new issues here at home, and I was becoming more involved in my community project at the intersection. Some days I would bring Jean along in the car, where she watched me and listened to music. One day the car battery went dead, which necessitated a call to the AAA. Earlier this year, Jean was walking down the street to see me when she fell on the pavement, breaking her left elbow. Two weeks after surgery, it had to be redone as it was not holding together. I was leery about having her going under anesthesia after what had happened following her leg surgery last year.

The New Century

In the latter part of 2004, my niece, Sue Marinzel, showed me a picture of President Clinton standing near a case for displaying commemorative coins. She asked me to make such a case for Eddie, her husband, who was the top-level Secret Service man in the White House. I fashioned an item the best I could out of some black walnut, which I had on hand. While I worked on Eddie's case, I mentioned to Jean that President Bush may have use for one as well, and we came to the conclusion that a second case was a good idea. In the end, I had two identical cases with engraved brass nameplates identifying the proposed owners. When Eddie was presented his case after Christmas, he was generous in his praise of my creation. I then pointed to a second carton and told him there was a like case in it for President George W. Bush.

"That is wonderful," he said. "I will give it to him tomorrow."

I was excited to hear his reply. I told him I had included a personal note inside the carton.

The following is a copy of my note:

Dear President Bush,

My niece, Eddie Marinzel's wife, asked me to make him a case for displaying commemorative coins which he had accumulated over a period of time. She gave me a picture of President Clinton standing near such an item in the Oval office filled with coins. I thought if former President Clinton and Eddie had use for such

Charles F. Remaley Jr.

a case you could use one as well. So, here it is, one of
a pair in existence. I offer it to you out of gratitude for
your service to our nation and with heartfelt joy over your
reelection to serve us for four more years. Congratulations!
God Bless You!

Respectfully yours,
Pastor Charles F. Remaley, Jr.

Early in January I received the following reply from President
George W. Bush:

**THE WHITE HOUSE
WASHINGTON**

January 3, 2005
The Reverend Charles F. Remaley, Jr.

Dear Reverend Remaley:

Eddie Marinzel passed along your kind note and
handsome challenge coin display case. Thank you for
your thoughtful gift.

Laura joins me in sending our best wishes for health
and happiness in the new year.

I have had the pleasure of meeting your niece Susie
several times, and I know how proud you must be of
her. She is a patient soul to put up with the long hours and
difficult schedule that Eddie has to keep. Laura and I are
most grateful to her and to the kids for their sacrifice.

Sincerely,
(Signed)
George W. Bush

Eddie told me President Bush had the case in his library at his Crawford, Texas, ranch.

When Jean and I arrived home from church today, there were balloons all over the place throughout our yard and porch. Here, in October 2005, Jean and I were marking our eightieth birthdays, and we had just been informed by Carol and Bob that they were having a birthday party for us, beginning in an hour. All of a sudden, people began arriving, some whom we had just talked with at church—cousins from East Brady, many neighbors, my friend the chief of police for our community, Jack and Mamie Felger from Ohio, other relatives, and real surprise guests, Bob and Pat Friend. Earlier in these writings, I mentioned being at the 1960 World Series when Bill Mazeroski hit his series-winning home run against the New York Yankees. Well, our guest Bob Friend had pitched for the Pittsburgh Pirates in that series. Jean and I were just overwhelmed at how our kids were able to pull this off without us being suspicious. We had such a good time and felt so blessed and honored to have such a grand party, a day never to be forgotten. Lisa, my sister-in-law, and brother Bud put together a photo album containing pictures of me from back in my childhood up into recent times. They put a heading on it: "This Is Your Life." What a remarkable gift. Two of the pictures showed Jean and me on the turf at Forbes Field with the scoreboard in the background displaying the winning results of game seven in the 1960 World Series.

During my youth, I spent much time at the swimming pool in Oakmont and many days caddying at the local country club. Along with all that exposure to the sun, add those many months in the South Pacific, and you have a recipe for skin cancer. Well, I had it big time. I had dozens of cancers removed, plus two bouts with melanoma, but I was doing well under the care of a good surgeon, Dr. John Zitelli.

Lately, Jean had been having a more difficult time getting in and out of the bathtub. To help her, I purchased an electric bath chair, which would lower her into the water and raise her out. It was battery supplied, so there was no danger of shock. She really did not like this chair, but it was the safest thing I could think of.

My brother, Bud, had some nasty falls in recent months and then a car crash here in 2006. Each fall had taken a toll on him, and the car accident may have given him a concussion. However, he had been back in his dental office and recently repaired a tooth for Jean. As we were leaving his office, we had a good talk. He seemed fine to us around 3:30 p.m. that day, but that evening he suffered a massive stroke and showed no signs of coming out of it. He passed away in mid-December. Now Jean and I each had only a sister left in each of our immediate families.

After a heavy rain and windstorm, I took Jean to her beauty salon. I would always wait in the car, listening to music. She got out of the car and my eyes did not follow her. In a moment, I heard her scream, and as I looked up, she was horizontal in midair four feet above a concrete landing. She had ascended three concrete steps onto the narrow stoop by the salon door and grabbed at the large, aluminum, flange–type door handle. The flange was still wet from the rain, and her hand had slipped off. Since the stoop was too narrow for Jean to regain her balance, she had ended in midair—then plunged onto the concrete. I only took a moment to reach her. She was conscious and speaking to me. I rushed in the door and told the beautician to call 911. The ambulance arrived quickly. Jean had a large lump on the back of her head. Having been horizontal in her fall, I can only believe it had allowed for an even distribution of her weight at impact, for she had no broken bones and the MRI of her head showed no signs of injury. Thank God!

I hoped this was not a tip-off as to what 2007 was going to be like. We really had a good year and continued going out to lunch two or three times a week. For years, we had been going to the Oakhurst Tea Room in Somerset County, twice a week, a distance of fifty-seven miles each way. We always dined there with friends, sometimes as many as ten at our table.

With the help of my cousin, Miles Humphrey, we fashioned seven planters out of four-by-six-inch timbers and installed them at the nearby intersection. The planters were two feet by eight feet and were now filled with a mix of beautiful flowers, with a mugho pine shrub in the center of each bed. It sure brightened our neighborhood. I had a discarded shopping cart that held nine gallons of water, and I would push it to the corner most days to freshen the flowers. A nice lawn was developing on the entire site. It kept me busy, and many people stopped to give me an "Atta boy." It was good for the ego.

On a January 2009 Sunday morning, Jean and I were seated on the sofa just before our departure time for church. As Jean stood up, she stumbled and fell to the floor. She was in great pain, so I called 911 for an ambulance. She was diagnosed with a fractured right hip. Carol flew in from Georgia for the operation. After the surgery, and while Jean was still in recovery, the surgeon summoned Carol, Bob, and me to a room off the waiting room. He explained that the surgery, which involved the placing of two steel rods in her hip, and her advanced age (eighty-four) gave her little chance of surviving much beyond a year. He was sympathetic and honest about what he believed. This was crushing news, but did not panic us, for we knew Jean was a woman of faith and a fighter. She spent several weeks in rehabilitation and came home using a walker, but could not climb stairs, so we rented a hospital bed for night use. We converted our dining room into a bedroom, as there was a connecting bathroom. Jean had a marvelous recovery in that she was walking on her own and climbing stairs. I added another handrail for ease and safety. I was confident in her future.

Last year, our lovely daughter-in-law, Debbie, was dismissed from her office job without a sound reason, which was in October 2008. In December, Bob called me one evening, telling me about some things he observed about Debbie, such as dropping things and having some near falls. He said he would be taking her to the doctor next morning. I suggested going straight to the hospital. When the doctor examined Debbie the next morning, he had her rushed to the hospital, where it was confirmed that she had a brain tumor. She was operated on to remove the tumor, followed by all manner of tests and invasive procedures. Bob knew early on, through conferences with Debbie's surgeon, that they were buying time with each procedure and that time was running out.

Debbie's mother, Pat Doege, lived three blocks away from Deb and Bob, and it became apparent that staying with her mom was the only solution to this ongoing battle. Each morning Bob arrived early at Pat's home to help get Debbie's day started, then headed out to work. And he returned in the evening to spend time with her. After many months and numerous trips to the hospital, her life was ebbing away. On the morning of September 24, 2009, Bob entered her room only to discover that, without having aroused her mother, Debbie, at age fifty-five, had passed away. There was no describing our loss. She was such a joy. She had such a beautiful voice and sang in our church choir for most of her life alongside of her mother. Deb and Bob were so truly happy, and we could sense the heartache and void in Bob's life.

It had been overwhelming with Debbie's diagnosis in December 2008, Jean's broken hip in January 2009, and then in April 2009, Carol had been diagnosed with breast cancer. She was in Atlanta, Georgia, where she and her husband had lived since 1991. Carol was fortunate it had been caught early, and had surgery twice during the period of May through September.

Over the years, we held many *LST-1024* reunions, in many cities from St. Louis to Philadelphia and from Boston to Panama City, Florida. In 2010, Andy and Shelly Carter, daughter and son-in-law of Mamie and Jack Felger, agreed to take control of this year's reunion. This year's get-together was to be held in Pittsburgh, so they asked me to choose a motel handy to the airport yet near the city. Jean and I set out to find such a location and ended up choosing a fine motel in an area called Greentree. This was well received by the Carters and all who attended the reunion. We did not settle any world affairs, we just had a good time. In Pittsburgh, I believe the highlight for the crew and families was riding the inclines that went up and down the steep slopes of Mount Washington, near the church area where I had served as pastor. Normally we closed our reunions with a banquet, but Jean and I volunteered to have everyone come to our home for a picnic supper before their trips back to their homes. We had a grand time in hosting this affair, which turned out to be the last reunion Jean and I were able to attend. At this writing, we only know of three surviving shipmates. The last to pass away was, my dear friend, Jack Felger.

This journey I am on, which I share with you, is at times like a poorly kept diary, as I tend to skip a year here and there. The further into this journey I go, the less there is to tell as Father Time takes his toll. Jean and I no longer took off to visit Carol and Lynn in Georgia. In fact, the last visit was accomplished because Bob was able to go along as chief driver. There were no further trips to Glen Ellyn, Illinois. On the twenty-fourth of June this year, our brother-in-law, Jim Beers, passed away. He and Jane had been living in a nice retirement home. Jim had, over time, had some mini strokes, and along with his dementia, it was all his body could take. He and Jane had been married sixty-four years.

On March 6 of this year (2013) I was out with my large snow thrower cleaning up a heavy snow in four of my neighbors' driveways. Then I did my own before heading next door to do Phil Giuffre's driveway. As I was plowing along the curb, my snow thrower chute jammed with snow. When this would happen, I always took my hands off the controls, which allowed the engine to run but stopped the rotating blades. Then I would push the snow down in or pull it up out of the chute, which I had been doing for nineteen years. Well, the blades did not stop turning and smashed my left hand as I pushed down on the snow. I saw quite plainly what had happened, but instantly gave thanks that it was my left hand, and then thought about the Wounded Warriors who have no hands. These are the facts, then: instead of leaving the machine in the street, I turned it around and drove it back to my driveway before shutting it down. Then I hollered in the door to Jean to call Michael, whose driveway I had just cleared. I needed him to call Bob to come immediately, as Jean with her dementia could not do what needed to be done. Bob called for an ambulance and made the decision as to which trauma unit I should go to. He chose the Presbyterian Hospital in Pittsburgh. Three of my fingers were dangling lifelessly when the surgeon, Dr. Alexander Spies, came on the scene. He had been called in from another hospital. In his résumé, he was known to have done some hand transplants.

Before the surgery, the doctor sat down to explain what he could do for me. He said he could not save the middle finger, but would do all that was possible to save the other two. My thumb and little finger were not injured. When I awoke from the surgery, my hand was wrapped in an enormous bandage with the tips of three fingers and a thumb visible at the end. Praise God! The doctor had put the fingers together and placed pins in them.

I had pretty good use of my left hand, and I was missing only half of the middle finger. I was truly blessed to have such a talented surgeon. You may not appreciate this, but I must tell it anyway. In talking to a friend when the next snow fell, she said, "Do not do what you did last time."

I replied, "I would not have the finger to do it again."

You know, you just cannot lose your sense of humor, nor your sense of gratitude. Daughter Carol wanted to be with me during this ordeal, but could not come because she had undergone a hip-replacement operation less than ten days before my mishap. She was under the watchful care of husband Lynn.

For Carol and me, it was good to put 2013 behind us and hope for less painful experiences in 2014. In the new year, Jean and I continued our routine of going out to lunch at least twice a week to the Oakhurst Tea Room. For many years we had done this, meeting with friends, who had been strangers to us in our earlier visits, but we were drawn to each other over time. Our common bond was that we liked Oakhurst and a good buffet lunch, but did not know a great deal about each other's backgrounds in those early years. One of these dear friends was Warren Enfield, a retiree from Gulf Oil. Warren was a quiet man who dressed casually, drove a small, inexpensive car, and had a good sense of humor. One day he told us he was going to give his church some money, as they had just moved into a new building. I knew the Sunday on which he was going to give the money, so I called him that evening to ask how things went. He told me the congregation gave him a standing ovation, cheered him, and hugged him. I shared in his joy, but had no idea what he contributed to his church. A few days later, in the Somerset newspaper, there was an article headlined "Local Man Gives $500,000 to His Church." Wow, what a wonderful way to learn a little more about a friend. We lost this dear friend at the age of ninety-eight. We truly miss him.

On the first Saturday in August, we held our Remaley reunion. Each year, the attendance got smaller. This year set a record with only thirteen present, and while we had a good time, we voted to abandon this yearly event. The following day, Sunday, after church, Jean was upstairs by herself when I heard a loud thump. I rushed up the stairs to find her on the floor. She had broken her back in that fall. She was rushed to the hospital. A specialist, Dr. Silvaggio, was called in from his home. The situation was one that if she did not have surgery, she could die, and if she had the surgery, it could kill her. I guess we were between a rock and a hard place. We were discussing the love of my life's future. I had to give the okay for the operation. After many hours in surgery, I was informed about what was done to Jean. There was a fusion of discs, and then along each side of her spine, steel rods were inserted. The opening was twelve to fourteen inches long. The prognosis for this operation on an eighty-nine-year-old person with dementia was not good, but she was in God's hands and we would keep the vigil.

Jean survived the operation, and after several days was transferred to the Presbyterian SeniorCare facility in Oakmont for rehabilitation. I became more and more confident that Jean would get well enough to come back home, so I had electric chairlifts installed on both sets of stairs. I also knew I could continue to be her caregiver, such as I had been for many years. We were so in love and just had to be together.

I had been visiting Jean twice daily for a month at the nursing home. She had been released into my care here at home. I had much to learn about caring for her in this condition, as she had to use a walker or wheelchair in the house. Her spirit was remarkably good, which made for a better patient. The chairlifts were a blessing because she could not climb the stairs. We were getting back to our lunch routine, but we only went to the Oakhurst Tea Room once weekly instead of the usual two trips. It was a real problem for me when she had to use the ladies room after the long drive. Occasionally, one of our friends helped, but with some of the "accidents" she had in the restroom, they shied away, which I could understand. Best of all, we were together, and so in love after sixty-eight years.

Escaping into another year, Jean and I were doing very well. However, sister Jane, who had been in a skilled nursing facility since the day husband Jim had died, passed away on June 17, 2015. She had been fed through a tube all this time, so she had not had a pleasant time. I told Jean her twin sister had died, but it did not register, as she continued to talk as though both Jim and Jane were still alive.

Our son-in-law, Lynn, had been in and out of the hospital numerous times since last year. He and Carol had been here for this past Christmas and he seemed well to us, but after going back home, it seemed something else was happening every time he turned around. For example, he spent fifty days in the hospital and rehab due to severe intestinal bleeding. Later, he had a heart attack in the doctor's office while Carol stood next to him, and then his replaced aortic heart valve began to fail after only four years. Carol named so many things from which Lynn was suffering. Nobody could say why he was suffering so much. Lynn was a decorated veteran in the Vietnam War, serving with the Green Berets. He was a fine golfer and could hit off the tee nearly three hundred yards, double what I was doing. That is probably the reason he always won our matches. You may recall, from earlier writings in this book, that I performed their marriage in 1969, nearly forty-six years ago. Sadly, Lynn passed away on October 30, 2015, at the age of sixty-seven and was buried with military honors at the Georgia National Cemetery. Jean and I had suffered the loss of both of our in-law children, but those losses were even greater to our children.

We were left without a choice as we moved into 2016, praying for a good year. All was going well until one day in March. Jean and I had just come into our basement from the garage. I sat Jean on the chairlift and warned her that the door at the top of the stair was closed tightly. It was usually left ajar. She rode the lift up the stairs and allowed her right wrist to hang over the side of the arm rest. In that position, it jammed against the door, fracturing it. Bob and I took Jean to an urgent-care center in Monroeville. In addition to the fracture, there were two other places on her arm where the skin peeled back as a flap. The doctor sewed up the skin and then read the x-rays. She chose not to operate, but to place Jean's wrist in a brace for six weeks, allowing removal for washing.

Being right handed, this made everything more difficult than things had been before the fracture, especially at potty time, as Jean was of little help to herself even then. But where there is a will, there is a way, and together we coped with whatever turned up for a period of five weeks when the doctor removed the brace. After eating left handed during those weeks, she continued to eat left handed without the brace.

I did not get much time to retrain Jean to use her right hand, because on the morning of May 1, 2016, she told me she felt light headed and that her whole world was spinning. Another call to 911 brought the ambulance to our door with another trip to the hospital. For five days, they ran every conceivable test on Jean, but found nothing wrong other than her dementia. They decided to send her back to Presbyterian SeniorCare, in the Willows unit, for therapy. After a few days, I could see that Jean's condition was deteriorating and mentioned my observation to the social worker. She was well aware of what I was seeing. She told me there was one vacancy in their dementia department and asked if I wanted to look at the room. When I looked out the window from that fourth-floor room, the view was of the world-famous Oakmont Country Club. I felt that if Jean were to spend the rest of her life here, she deserved a good view. I said, "Put Jean's name on this room." The next day, she was moved into that room. We spent a lot of time looking out that window, holding hands while taking in the view. I loved her so.

In all my life, I had never seen more tender, loving care than what I witnessed here at the Willows. You might expect that one aide or nurse would rise above the others in dishing out TLC, but here it was shown by all. I could not be more confident that Jean was in the right hands. In my gratitude, I often hugged one of these angels.

Speaking of gratitude, I looked back to the year 2003 when Jean's family doctor, Barbara Kevish, first put her on medications for dementia. Had they cured the ailment? No! Had they prolonged Jean's life? Only God knows. But with gratitude in my heart, I believe the medications gave Jean a better life over these thirteen years during which she had taken them, so I am deeply grateful to Dr. Kevish, who treated Jean with love and friendship.

As I approached the threshold where I might lose the love of my life, I reflected upon what the doctor told us following the surgery in 2009 on Jean's right hip. He had told us that the seriousness of the operation and Jean's age might give her as little as one year to live. Then in 2014, after her major spinal surgery, the surgeon and Dr. Kevish had marveled at Jean's survival. In fact, Dr. Kevish had called Jean the "Miracle Lady." I felt that we had seven "bonus years" together in spite of the odds against us. I truly praise God. The road had not been easy, but it had been love filled and blessed.

Jean was on an unrestricted diet and was eating well. With dementia, it is not unusual for a patient to refuse to eat, and Jean had such spells but was okay now. I would go with her to the dining room for lunch and dinner and help in cutting her meat or getting something to drink. Many of the patients were unable to help themselves, so at mealtime there were nurses and aides to feed them. They showed so much patience in this task.

The rooms here were singles with a shared bathroom with one other patient. Eleanor Kuhn was Jean's neighbor and was so nice. We became like family with Eleanor's daughters, Debbie, Kathy, and Marianne, along with sons-in law Dave and Joe. We leaned on each other and did some hugging. We were blessed. After Jean had broken her back, I had purchased an electric reclining chair, which not only reclined the patient, but stood them up! I brought that chair to the Willows for Jean to use in her room.

Under these trying circumstances, with the urging of my family, I returned to that Friday trip to the Oakhurst Tea Room. It was such a help to me. So as not to abandon Jean, I helped her with breakfast and then returned for her evening meal. I was so thankful for the good health I had, which had afforded me the privilege of caring for Jean. Otherwise, we probably both would have been together in a nursing home.

On this same floor where Jean was located, there was a friend, Louise Rearick, the sister-in-law of Jack Rearick, the man who had joined me in the late 1940s in sponsoring that group of young boys in the Verona school. Louise had known me all my life. On October 19, she would celebrate her one hundredth birthday, the same day I would be celebrating my ninety-first birthday. I visited Louise every day. She still recognized me.

Carol came in from Georgia today (June 28) to keep the vigil with me for several days. Jean had been rather listless in the past few days, and with some blood work it was determined that she was in need of some intravenous medications not available at the Willows. She was at Saint Margaret's Hospital getting the necessary care. Yesterday, Dr. Dana Brown, my personal care physician, was on hospital-calls duty. After checking Jean's status, he turned to Carol and me and, at some length, spelled out her dire condition and that we must realize where she was in this life and what we were realistically facing in the near future. We deeply appreciated him for his heartfelt appraisal and for being so frank with us.

After a few days at the hospital with Jean, it was comforting to be back at the Willows. Over the weeks here, on this special floor, I had bonded with several people, but there were two other men keeping a vigil with their wives, just as I was. We had drawn close to each other in support of the others' days of travail. It was not so much what was said between us, it was the presence of three men sharing similar loads. Wesley Posvar had already been here with Palmer, his wife, when Jean arrived as a patient. He worked during the day and got here in time to feed her the evening meal. She lit up the moment he arrived and kissed her and expressed his love. She could only respond with a smile.

Jim Ruck was the other part of this trio, keeping a watchful vigil over his wife, Gail. Jim, being retired, was here nearly all day, every day, so we got to support each other at great length. I was so blessed to have these two men holding me up on days when they knew Jean's situation was a little worse.

Jean was eating fairly well on an unrestricted diet, but when she returned to the Willows, her diet was changed. All her food was pureed. This was done out of fear that her food would not find its proper way into her stomach. However, she did not take to this new way and gradually was eating less. I struggled mightily at each meal trying to feed her. She loved tomato soup, so when she refused to eat, I would ask one of the aides for some soup, which she would consume immediately. Day by day, Jean was getting weaker and thinner and could hardly talk above a whisper.

I placed another call to Georgia for Carol to come back. For these past four days, Jean had barely eaten anything at all, and after each meal wanted back in bed, where she would fall asleep. When Carol, Bob, and I left Jean's room last evening, she was near exhaustion, but fell asleep after saying she loved me. I told her of my love for her.

At seven this morning, August 5, 2016, I received a phone call from the Willows telling me that Jean, the love of my life, had passed away, forty days shy of seventy years of wedded bliss. I loved her with my whole being, and I know, in my heart, that she loved me in like manner. We were one in holy matrimony and one in Jesus Christ. I know where Jean is and that her days of suffering are over, and that she lives in eternal peace with our Lord.

The End

At the age of ninety-one, my journey may not be over, but I know it is nearing its end for time is running out. One might ask, "What is the high point of your journey?" A difficult question to answer, without telling my love story, but there is a core value at the heart of this journey. It is about a promise kept. A young soldier in full battle gear, Art Uhleman, climbed to my battle station on a forty-millimeter antiaircraft gun during the WWII Leyte invasion in the Philippines. The date was October 20, 1944. Art asked if I would write to him, and I quickly answered in the affirmative. He handed me a folded matchbook cover saying that his address was inside. We shook hands, he descended the ladder, and he was gone, to join in the assault on the beach.

When I opened the matchbook cover, I discovered that Art had written what I had guessed was his home address, for reasons known only to him. I had no choice but to write to that address, only to receive a letter from his mother telling me her only son had died in battle. I had kept my promise, but had not expected this outcome. The letter from Mrs. Uhleman was followed by a letter from a grieving young lady named Jean Simpson, explaining who she was—Art's fiancée—professing her love for him, and stating that nobody could take his place. She asked questions about Art, which due to censorship, I could not answer. However, I wrote to her, finding it difficult to choose the right words, as I did in writing to Art's mother.

Having kept a promise is part and parcel of this one man's journey. Without keeping that promise, only God knows what would have been the heart of my journey. In these writings, I have detailed my love story, and by the grace of God, it was a place in Jean's heart. We were never uncomfortable talking about Art. On our wedding day, Jean wore a cross on a gold chain around her neck, a gift from Art. When she was laid to rest, she wore that same cross. Love is all encompassing.

In bringing these writings to a close, I think about the last formal sermon I preached. Its title was "That's Life." Well, this has been one man's journey—that's life!